TODAY WITH ISAIAH

Volume 1

D1419925

Clifford Hill

The Centre for Biblical and Hebraic Studies

Other books in the series:

Today with Jeremiah – Volume 1

Copyright © The Centre for Biblical and Hebraic Studies 1999

Published by
The Centre for Biblical and Hebraic Studies,
a ministry of PWM Trust (Charity Number 326533)

First published 1999

Unless otherwise indicated, biblical quotes are from the
New International Version © 1973, 1978, 1984
by the International Bible Society.

ISBN: 1 872395 60 0

British Library Cataloguing in Publication Data.
A catalogue record for this book is available from the British Library.

Printed by Cox and Wyman, Reading, England

Manuscript typed by Ruth Addington, Jean Wolton and Gillian Orpin

Typeset by Andrew Lewis

TODAY WITH ISAIAH

FOREWORD

The Bible reveals a considerable degree of ambivalence toward those who claim to exercise a prophetic ministry (eg 2 Chronicles 20: 20; cf Jeremiah 23: 28). The reason is not hard to understand, for no other ministry is more important for the well-being of God's people, and no other ministry is so vulnerable to unintentional subjectivity or open to wilful abuse.

To the prophet is given the awesome responsibility of speaking forth the authoritative word of the Lord, and yet his message is subject to so many checks and balances before the prophetic word is given the seal of authenticity. No wonder then that in both the biblical record and in the experience of the church, self-styled prophets come and go with amazing rapidity.

Isaiah's long ministry of more than forty years, witnessing to the constancy of the 'Holy One of Israel' in the midst of some of the greatest ups and downs of Israel's story, have great relevance for our day where immediacy and conformity to the ever-changing 'spirit of the age' are the norms of our society.

The fact that Isaiah was able to sustain that ministry from a position close to the centre of Israel's leadership is surely a challenge for us in an age where counter-establishment protests have almost become of the essence of the so-called 'prophetic voice'.

In the light of this, perhaps no-one is in a better position to relate Isaiah's message to our daily lives than Clifford Hill. His prophetic ministry to our nation, though perhaps still short in years compared with Isaiah's life-long ministry, has been always relevant and consistent through a period of rapid and deep changes in the foundational thinking and practical life-style of our so-called 'first-world' community of peoples.

In all this, through the 'Prophetic Word Ministries' which he founded in 1983, and in which the Centre of Biblical and Hebraic Studies has been birthed, Dr Hill has sought to speak for 'The Holy One of Israel'. The fact that his message has been seen as relevant and authentic, if not always popular, has given him openings for a wider input in important matters relating to our national life, not least regarding support for biblical family values which are at a critical stage in today's society.

The essence of the New Covenant, which of course is permeated by the whole of the Hebrew Scriptures, is perhaps seen more obviously in the prophecy of Isaiah than elsewhere in those writings. And, of course, many have become acquainted with this book through the well-known portions that are read at Carol Services and through its major input to Handel's 'Messiah'. But there may be many in the churches today for whom Isaiah is best known for these extracts, and for whom the fuller reading of such a work is almost too daunting to undertake.

This book will enrich the lives of all who seek a renewal and enlargement of faith, by allowing Isaiah to speak anew into the daily experiences of personal life.

John Fieldsend
November 1999

PREFACE

The Book of Isaiah

The book of Isaiah is, by any standard, a treasure trove of spiritual riches. In the Hebrew Bible it is given the foremost place in the section known as 'The Latter Prophets'. This consists of four rolls, namely Isaiah, Jeremiah, Ezekiel and The Twelve. The latter are known in English as 'The Minor Prophets' because of the brevity of their writings rather than the authority of their preaching.

The Book of Isaiah is more of a library than a single book. It has no continuity or single theme running right the way through, but rather is a mixture of prose and poetry with many different subjects covered. These consist of a collection of prophecies and narrative, which have reference to different events and circumstances but which, when understood, give wonderful spiritual insight into the word of God conveyed through the prophets to his people.

In order to understand the message it is necessary to know the background, the culture and the idioms of the day in which the word of God was conveyed to the people. When these are unravelled the spiritual gems are revealed. This is what is attempted in these readings in Isaiah.

The prophecies we shall be examining come from the Eighth Century BC and originated through the ministry of the man we know as Isaiah of Jerusalem. Both he and Jeremiah, some 120 years later, had long ministries of more than 40 years. It is generally believed that Isaiah's call to ministry occurred in the year 744 BC and he is known to have been still in active ministry in the year 700 BC and possibly early into the new century.

Isaiah was the leader of a group of disciples. It may be that he gathered them around him in reaction to the refusal of King Ahaz to heed the word of the Lord that the prophet had declared. It was probably around this time that Isaiah began to see that the hope of the nation lay in a remnant rather than in the whole nation acting as the servant of the Lord. He looked for repentance and absolute trust in the Lord but saw little or no sign of any turning in the nation. It is at this point in his ministry that we find Isaiah speaking of binding up his testimony and sealing his teaching among his disciples (8: 16). He follows this with the statement, 'I will wait for the Lord, who is hiding his face from the house of Jacob. I will put my trust in him.'

Isaiah's disciples would have been responsible for preserving the collection of his oracles, or sayings, as well as his prophecies concerning the future. They would have written them on scrolls and preserved them within what became known as the 'Isaianic school of prophecy'. This company of prophets remained in being for a long time after the death of Isaiah of Jerusalem.

There are three main sections to the Book of Isaiah as we have it today. These are chapters 1-39, 40-54 and 55-66. Our concern in this volume is with the first part of the Book of Isaiah. Even within that first part there are different sections which are quite clearly seen, even in reading our English translations. For example, there are prophecies concerning other nations. Chapters 36-39 are historical narrative which is paralleled in 2 Kings 18 and 2 Chronicles 32. Another section that is quite distinct is chapters 24-27 which is known as the 'Little Apocalypse' because of its eschatological content.

The major advantage in working through Isaiah in small sections as daily readings, is that we are not looking for continuity but rather opening up the word of the Lord as it would have been understood by those who first heard it declared in the Eighth Century BC. The amazing thing about the word of God is its timelessness and its relevance for us today.

Historical Background

Isaiah of Jerusalem prophesied during the reigns of Uzziah, Jotham, Ahaz and Hezekiah – that is, throughout the second half of the Eighth Century. This was a period of tremendous upheaval on the international front and political turmoil within Israel and Judah.

Isaiah 6 records the prophet's call to ministry which he says occurred in the year Uzziah died. This is variously reckoned to be between 744 BC and 740 BC, with the most likely date being 744 BC. The difficulty lies in knowing how long Jotham acted as Regent for his father, who was a leper, and how long he reigned in his own right. It is fairly well established that Ahaz began his reign in 741 BC, on the death of Jotham.

On the international scene Tiglath Pileser ruled Assyria from 745 BC to 727 BC. His first few years were spent in consolidating his own base in Mesopotamia but in 738 BC he moved west and, for the next century, Assyria dominated the whole region. Throughout that time there was constant rivalry between Assyria and Egypt but the little independent states of Syria, Israel, Judah, Philistia, Phoenicia, Edom, Moab and Ammon were caught up in the battle between the two great powers. One by one they were swallowed up into the great Assyrian Empire.

In 737 BC Pekah, King of Israel, formed an alliance with Resin, King of Syria, and they tried to force Judah into a coalition whose combined armies might have been capable of resisting the onslaught of the Assyrian forces. Judah refused to join the alliance whereupon the two kings threatened to invade Judah in order to replace Ahaz with a king more likely to comply with their wishes. The people of Judah were greatly shaken (7: 2) but Isaiah was happy with a policy of independence and strongly counselled Ahaz not to be anxious nor to lose heart (7: 4). Isaiah's counsel was total trust in God, but that was not what Ahaz had in mind. Instead, he sent to Assyria for help. Tiglath Pileser was only too pleased to comply and it was an added bonus that Ahaz actually paid him to attack his neighbours. In order to do this, Ahaz stripped gold and silver treasures from the Temple and from his own palace and sent them as a gift to Nineveh.

Assyria overran Syria, conquering Damascus in 734 BC, and the following year deposed Pekah and installed Hoshea as a puppet king in Israel. Assyria also deported large numbers of the population of Israel and scattered them across other provinces of the Empire in order to destroy national identity and reduce the risk of revolt.

After the death of Tiglath Pileser in 727 BC, revolts broke out among the small independent states, probably inspired by Egypt. In 724 BC Assyria struck, capturing and killing Hoshea. Samaria held out for three years of siege but eventually fell in 721 BC to Sargon who had succeeded Shalmaneser V in 722 BC.

Meanwhile, Hezekiah had come to the throne of Judah (720 BC) and there was a further attempt among the smaller states of Philistia, Edom and Moab to form an alliance against Assyria. Once again Isaiah stepped onto the forefront of the political stage and urged the king to have nothing to do with such a treaty. In fact, Isaiah went around Jerusalem barefoot and almost naked 'as a sign and portent against Egypt'. He said that it was in this manner that 'the King of Assyria will lead away stripped and barefoot the Egyptian captives' (20: 3-4). Once again

Isaiah's message was not to trust in other nations, or indeed to put any trust in people, but to trust in the Lord alone.

Sargon, who exceeded even the cruelty of his predecessors for ruthless tyranny, utterly destroyed Ashdod in 711 BC and he claims to have defeated an Egyptian army around this time. Judah escaped by paying tribute but, on the death of Sargon and the accession of Sennacherib in 705 BC, Hezekiah decided it was time to assert his independence. The only western vassal who remained faithful to Assyria was King Padi of Ekron, but he was deposed by his own subjects and sent to Jerusalem to be kept as a prisoner by Hezekiah. Isaiah unhesitatingly denounced Hezekiah for getting involved in international politics instead of trusting the Lord.

In 701 BC, Sennacherib ransacked the whole of Judah destroying all her fortified towns. When he was besieging Lachish, the last city before turning his full might upon Jerusalem, Hezekiah paid a huge tribute to save his capital city (2 Kings 18: 14).

Despite this, Sennacherib decided to attack Jerusalem. He sent a threatening letter saying that none of the gods of the other nations had been able to save their lands and that the Lord would be equally powerless: 'Who of all the gods of these countries has been able to save his land from me? How then can the Lord deliver Jerusalem from my hand?' (36: 20).

Isaiah saw this as a direct insult to God. While the King spread the letter out before the Lord in the Temple (37: 14), Isaiah prophesied the downfall of Sennacherib (2 Kings 19: 20f). As a consequence, 'that night the angel of the Lord went out and put to death 185,000 men in the Assyrian camp' (2 Kings 19: 35). The plague that swept through the Assyrian army forced Sennacherib to withdraw and

11

Jerusalem was saved.

This is the last we hear of the great prophet Isaiah, as the account in Isaiah 39 of the envoys coming from Babylon is generally thought to have occurred just prior to Sennacherib's invasion of Judah. The whole of his ministry was therefore dominated by the conflict with Assyria.

Social and Religious Situation

The great Eighth Century prophets – Amos and Hosea in the Northern Kingdom of Israel, and Micah and Isaiah in the Southern Kingdom of Judah – all reveal details of the social, moral and spiritual condition of the Hebrew people of that day. Their combined writings paint a picture of riches, luxury and indolence on the one hand, and of poverty, squalor and injustice on the other.

The first half of the Eighth Century was a period of great prosperity for both Israel and Judah. It was a time of political stability, with the long reign of Jeroboam II in the north coinciding with the long reign of Uzziah (also known as Amaziah) in the south. It was during this period that there arose a class of rich capitalists, merchants and land-owners who dominated the economic and the social order, and even religious life, throughout Israel and Judah. Solomon in all his glory was the model of the age.

The small peasant farmers gradually disappeared as powerful landowners expanded their territory. A series of failed harvests drove the small farmer to borrow from the money-lenders. At the due time the debt would be called in and, if the farmer could not pay, his land would be forfeited. If he needed further money to feed his family, first his children, and then the whole family, would be taken into slavery. They would continue to work the land but, while their lifestyle would be reduced to squalor, the rich would live in luxurious self-indulgence.

Isaiah and Amos were outstanding among the prophets in their condemnation of these practices. 'Woe to you who add house to house and join field to field till no space is left', thundered Isaiah. 'Surely the great houses will become desolate, the fine mansions left without occupants', he declared (5: 8-9).

The rich held the power and they used it to oppress the poor. Isaiah denounces those 'who acquit the guilty for a bribe, but deny justice to the innocent' (5: 23). He says God will bring judgment upon those who despise the poor and who live lives of indolent self-indulgence. 'Woe to those who rise early in the morning to run after their drinks, who stay up late at night till they are inflamed with wine' (5: 11).

In 3: 18-23, Isaiah describes the elaborate dress code of the rich, their adornments and finery. Such a society, he says, will inevitably have to come under God's judgment. Just as Amos told the people of Israel that the day of the Lord would be a day of darkness and not of light (Amos 5: 20), so Isaiah told the people of Judah that 'the Lord Almighty has a day in store for all the proud and lofty, for all that is exalted and they will be humbled' (2: 12).

God had heard the cries of the poor, the powerless and the oppressed. The day would come when he would release them from their bondage and punish the wickedness of those who ignored his warnings and despised his word.

Isaiah – The Man

As a young man, Isaiah must have heard of the prophets Amos and Hosea in the northern kingdom and we know from Jeremiah 26: 18 that Isaiah was a contemporary of Micah, who also prophesied in Judah during the reign of Hezekiah. But Micah was a countryman used to living and working among peasant farmers and this is reflected in his ministry. By contrast, Isaiah was a townsman, living and working in Jerusalem.

There are some indications that Isaiah himself came from a rich family or, at least, that his family origins were among the aristocracy of the day. Clearly he had status which enabled him to gain access to kings and to speak with the rulers of the nation. Many times his counsel went unheeded but he was, nevertheless, in a position to convey the word of God to those who exercised power in the nation. He was, thus, the ideal servant of the Lord for his day. He was utterly fearless and uncompromising in declaring the message that he had received in the council of God.

We know very little about Isaiah's personal life, but we do know that he was married, although we are not told anything about his wife's family background. Isaiah himself refers to his wife as a prophetess (8: 3). We also know that Isaiah gave his children 'prophetic names', such as Maher-Shalal-Hash-Baz, meaning 'quick to the plunder, swift to the spoil'. We also hear of a son named Shear-Jashub, meaning 'a remnant will survive'.

This practice of giving prophetic names was not uncommon among the prophets as we know from Hosea, who even called one of his children 'not mine' (which must have given rise to talk among the neighbours!). Hosea was emphasising God's rejection of his unfaithful people, just as Isaiah was warning of judgment falling upon a faithless people. He was expressing his conviction that the only hope for the future lay in the survival of a small remnant, which who would remain devoted to the Lord.

We do not know what happened to Isaiah in the end but there was a strong tradition passed down through the generations that he was murdered by Manasseh. The king reputedly took the elderly prophet, who had ministered to the nation faithfully for more than 40 years, and had him sawn in two. This Rabbinic tradition of the prophet's martyrdom is reflected in Hebrews 11: 37.

The Message

Isaiah's message through his long ministry was set against the background of international politics which were dominated by the constant threat from Assyria. On the home front it was the social, moral and spiritual state of the nation which was a constant sorrow for the prophet. He knew the love and faithfulness of the Lord who was a covenant-keeping God and who would guard and protect his people if they trusted him and were faithful to his word. But Isaiah knew the Lord to be a God of holiness who would not defend an unholy people.

Isaiah's message was influenced throughout his life by the revelation of God which he had received at the time of his call to ministry and anointing as a prophet. That experience is graphically described in Chapter 6 where the young Isaiah, probably during a time of prayer and meditation in the Temple, received a life-changing revelation of the divine nature and purposes.

His own unworthiness and uncleanness in the presence of the holiness of God made a lasting impression upon him. It was an awesome experience to enter into the presence of the Almighty, the creator of the ends of the universe. God's response was to bring forgiveness and cleansing, which was followed by the commissioning of the prophet.

W Elmslie refers to Isaiah's commission as establishing the foundation for the message which he carried throughout his ministry. He says that from this experience, *'three convictions were forever established in Isaiah's mind:*

First, he knew that the world and all that it contains is as naught beside the reality of God, who is its creator and controller.

Second, nothing that human strength effects could alter God's purpose or avert the end towards which he is directing history.

Third, Isaiah felt the splendour of God as measureless moral purity; and yet, in the very instant of his confession of sinfulness, knew himself to be, not only forgiven, but called and accepted by God into the service of the divine purpose.

From these three immutable beliefs his subsequent thought flowed as a river from its source' (W Elmslie, 'How Came Our Faith', Cambridge, 1948, p 292).

Isaiah's conviction of the sovereignty of God and of his absolute control over the affairs of the nations was foundational to his personal faith and to the ministry he exercised. He believed that if Israel and Judah, as the covenant people of God, were faithful, then they would be protected against all invaders. 'The Egyptians are men and not God', he declared, 'their horses are flesh and not spirit' (31: 3a). Therefore God's message to the nation was, 'Woe to those who go down to Egypt for help, who rely on horses, who trust in the multitude of their chariots... but do not look to the Holy One of Israel, or seek help from the Lord' (31: 1).

God's sovereign control over the nations was such that he would even use a pagan nation to bring judgment upon his own covenant people if they were disobedient and faithless. Hence Isaiah was able to declare, 'Woe to the Assyrian, the rod of my anger, in whose hand is the club of my wrath! I send him against a godless nation, I despatch him against a people who anger me' (10: 5-6a).

Isaiah nevertheless knew that the Assyrians had no understanding of being used to fulfil the purposes of God; Tiglath Pileser's purpose was quite different from the Lord's. Hence the prophet declared of the Assyrian, 'But this is not what he intends, this is not what he has in mind;

his purpose is to destroy, to put an end to many nations' (10: 5-7).

There is great consistency in Isaiah's message throughout his long ministry. He stood firmly against immorality, injustice, oppression and idolatry. These were all evidence of the sinfulness of the people, their wilful disregard of the word of God and the terms of their covenant relationship with the Lord. Like Jeremiah 120 years later, Isaiah pleaded with the leaders of the nation and the ordinary people to recognise the danger they were in, through their own folly, in not heeding the word of the Lord and not understanding his requirements.

As the international threat of invasion from Assyria grew, Isaiah maintained a steady witness saying that a simple trust in God was all that was required, together with righteous living. Like Jeremiah, he experienced the tragedy of having his message rejected, his warnings go unheeded and judgment befalling the nation as a consequence. 'This is what the Sovereign Lord, the Holy One of Israel, says: "In repentance and rest is your salvation, in quietness and trust is your strength, but you would have none of it. You said, 'No we will flee on horses.' Therefore you will flee!"' (30: 15-16).

Isaiah did have the joy of working with a good and faithful king, Hezekiah, under whose leadership much of the outward signs of idolatry were cleared from the nation and revival swept through Jerusalem, of which there is a graphic account in 2 Chronicles 30: 13 – 31: 1. He also had the joy of seeing the fulfilment of his own prophecy that the Assyrian army would be decimated by the Lord and Jerusalem would not fall into the hands of Sennacherib.

Isaiah nevertheless knew that the hearts of the people needed to be changed in every generation. He foresaw that, in the future, they would turn back to idolatry and their faithless ways which would eventually result in the Lord driving them out of the land into exile. This was the substance of Isaiah's final conversation with King Hezekiah recorded in Isaiah 39: 5-8.

So Isaiah, who was among the greatest of all Israel's seers, maintained a faithful witness to the Lord right to the end of his days. He carried the same message throughout his life, calling for a simple trust in the Lord, who was Israel's teacher and protector, who loved his people and longed to guide them. He said that if only they would listen to the Lord in simple love and trust, they would find that, 'whether you turn to the right or to the left, your ears will hear a voice behind you, saying, "This is the way; walk in it"' (30: 21).

This is a message that is still relevant today, for the Holy One of Israel, Father of our Lord Jesus the Messiah, is a God who keeps his promises!

Clifford Hill
November 1999

THE LOVE OF GOD

Isaiah 1: 2-4

Hear, O heavens! Listen, O earth! For the Lord has spoken: 'I reared children and brought them up, but they have rebelled against me. The ox knows his master, the donkey his owner's manger, but Israel does not know, my people do not understand.' Ah, sinful nation, a people loaded with guilt, a brood of evildoers, children given to corruption. They have forsaken the Lord; they have spurned the Holy One of Israel and turned their backs on him.

Comment:

This is one of those passages in which Isaiah touches the very heart of God. His own people, whom he had called into a covenant relationship with himself, had rebelled against him. The whole life of the nation in the closing years of Uzziah's reign reflected a people who had rejected the word of God. Isaiah was deeply concerned that, in the midst of the economic prosperity he saw all around him, there was moral and spiritual bankruptcy at the heart of the nation.

When the prophet got into the presence of the Lord he realised how much God was grieving over his people. God is love; and if we wish to know God we have to try to understand his immense and unsurpassable love.

John exclaims, 'How great is the love the Father has lavished upon us that we should be called the children of God!' (1 John 3: 1). Yet despite the incredible privilege we enjoy of being 'children of God' – his own dear, precious children – we so often turn our backs upon him.

This is what Israel had done and Isaiah is reflecting

God's deep sorrow and amazement that the children he had birthed and reared had rebelled against him. Those whom he had guarded, protected and upon whom he had lavished his love so abundantly had spurned his love. He called upon the heavens and the earth to witness such a monstrous deed as the rebellion of his own children.

Even the dumb animals, who can never know or express the depths of love, at least know their own master and are loyal to him. But those who are God's own children turn away from him.

We will never know, in this life, the grief we cause the Father by our lack of trust in him and our lack of love towards him.

If we, as human parents can suffer when our children are unresponsive to our love, how much more does God suffer!

Prayer

Loving Father, forgive us for our lack of love and our unresponsive hearts. Make us more like the kind of children you want us to be – understanding, appreciative, obedient, pleasing. Let your love overflow into me and through me this day.

FORMAL RELIGION

Isaiah 1: 10-13a

Hear the word of the Lord, you rulers of Sodom; listen to the law of our God, you people of Gomorrah! 'The multitude of your sacrifices – what are they to me?' says the Lord. 'I have more than enough of burnt offerings, of rams and the fat of fattened animals; I have no pleasure in the blood of bulls and lambs and goats. When you come to appear before me, who has asked this of you, this trampling of my courts? Stop bringing meaningless offerings!'

Comment:

This is one of the earliest of Isaiah's prophecies, probably in the last days of Uzziah's reign, or during the short, five-year reign of his son Jotham. It was the close of an era of great prosperity for the southern Kingdom of Judah. But prosperity had taken the nation away from a simple trust in God.

Wealth, worldly power and glory had produced a generation that relied on their own human strength and saw little need for God. Religion had become a formality to be observed with great pomp and ceremony but little spiritual sincerity.

Temple worship had become a demonstration of the nation's wealth and in this prophecy Isaiah pronounces God's verdict upon it. To the Lord the whole nation had become like Sodom and Gomorrah. 'I have more than enough of burnt offerings... I have no pleasure in the blood of bulls... Who has asked this of you?'

God is not impressed by our elaborate worship or by our outward show of piety. Jesus referred to this in his story of the publican and the Pharisee who each prayed, but one was talking to himself rather than to God. Much earlier, the prophet Samuel, when choosing Israel's king from among the sons of Jesse, had said, 'The Lord does not look at the things man looks at. Man looks at the outward appearance, but the Lord looks at the heart' (1 Samuel 16: 7).

It is all too easy for public worship to become cold and formal. Even when it is lively it can be meaningless to us unless we go to worship in the right spirit, a spirit of humility and simple trust in God.

Our hearts need to be right with God if we are to enter fully into an act of worship. We may be able to deceive others with our show of piety and our enthusiastic worship, but we can never deceive God.

Prayer

Father, I confess that there have been many times when I have brought a meaningless offering before you. My worship is sometimes formal and lacking in reality. Forgive me, Father, and draw me closer to you, that I may worship you in spirit and in truth.

AWAY WITH HYPOCRISY

Isaiah 1: 15-17

'When you spread out your hands in prayer, I will hide my eyes from you; even if you offer many prayers, I will not listen. Your hands are full of blood; wash and make yourselves clean. Take your evil deeds out of my sight! Stop doing wrong, learn to do right! Seek justice, encourage the oppressed. Defend the cause of the fatherless, plead the case of the widow.'

Comment:

This is another of Isaiah's earliest prophecies which reflects the affluence of the times and the gulf between rich and poor. In the great prosperity of Uzziah's reign, the rich grew richer and the poor grew poorer. Isaiah expresses God's abhorrence at the hypocrisy and injustice that characterised the nation in the early days of his ministry. Hence his strong words, 'Take your evil deeds out of my sight! Stop doing wrong, learn to do right!'

God hates injustice and oppression, but when it is compounded by hypocrisy, the pretence of righteousness and the outward show of religion, his anger bursts upon the heads of those who do such things. 'When you spread out your hands in prayer I will hide my eyes from you; even if you offer many prayers, I will not listen.'

This is surely the most devastating thing God can say, that he refuses to listen to the prayers of his people, but it is a measure of his outrage at the behaviour of his people. 'Seek justice, encourage the oppressed. Defend the cause of the fatherless, plead the case of the widow.'

Oppression is not simply the sin of dictators. We can all be petty oppressors by misusing the small amount of power we have in the family, at work, or even in the church. God wants us to put things right in the family, in the church, in the community; to heal those broken relationships; yes, even if it does mean humbling ourselves.

Jesus said, 'If you are offering your gift at the altar and there remember that your brother has something against you, leave your gift there in front of the altar. First go and be reconciled to your brother; then come and offer your gifts' (Matthew 5: 23-24).

Remember it is the meek who inherit the Kingdom, not the proud. The Lord loves those who come to him with a broken and contrite heart.

Prayer
Father, I long to be in a right relationship with you and to live in peace and harmony with all those close to me. Help me to mend broken relationships and to improve those with the people around me in daily life, that you may never hide your eyes from me or be ashamed of me.

THE CHOICE

Isaiah 1: 18-20

'Come now, let us reason together,' says the Lord.
'Though your sins are like scarlet, they shall be as white
as snow; though they are red as crimson, they shall be
like wool. If you are willing and obedient, you will eat
the best from the land; but if you resist and rebel, you
will be devoured by the sword.' For the mouth of the
Lord has spoken.

Comment:

This prophecy is also one of the earliest words given by
Isaiah. It must have been received soon after his
dramatic experience of God appearing to him in the Temple
in the last days of Uzziah's reign. The nation was enjoying
great prosperity and international power and prestige, but
the king was a leper.

Uzziah lived the life of a recluse being banned even
from worship in the Temple, while his son Jotham attended
to the affairs of state as his Regent. In this prophecy God
offers the nation a choice – repentance and forgiveness, or
rebellion and disaster.

Although he is the Lord God Almighty, maker of heaven
and earth, who could enforce his will, he does not act in
that way. Instead he graciously invites the people to reason
things out with him. If they are willing and obedient and
confess their sins which are like scarlet, he will wash them
away so that they will be as white as snow.

God's forgiveness is complete and enables his children
to stand in a right relationship with him. But if they are
unwilling, if they resist and rebel, he will remove his
covering of protection and allow them to be devoured by

their enemies.

'Though your sins are like scarlet, they shall be as white as snow.' This can also be taken as a metaphor of leprosy. The prophet no doubt had King Uzziah in mind. The little telltale patches of scarlet on the skin, that are the first signs of leprosy, soon become the full-blown disease, with the skin flaking white as snow and the hair turning like wool.

The warning signs were there clearly enough for all to see. Only God could heal the nation of the terminal disease of moral corruption that they had brought upon themselves through their contact with a corrupt world. If they repented, God would heal them, but if they persisted in sin then they would be 'devoured by the sword'.

The message is the same to us today, both in our national life, and as individuals. If we allow the values of the world to take a hold in our lives they will soon become a barrier to the Spirit of God. We cannot serve two masters. This was the warning Jesus gave to his disciples and it is his word to us today.

Prayer
Father, you are so gracious and full of mercy. My sins are like scarlet. They are ever before me. Help me to choose what is right, and thereby to experience your loving forgiveness and to be close to your side.

THE LAST DAYS

Isaiah 2: 2-3a

In the last days the mountain of the Lord's temple will be established as chief among the mountains; it will be raised above the hills, and all nations will stream to it. Many peoples will come and say, 'Come, let us go up to the mountain of the Lord, to the house of the God of Jacob. He will teach us his ways, so that we may walk in his paths.'

Comment:

This beautiful prophecy is repeated almost word for word in Micah 4. No-one knows which prophet actually received it. Isaiah and Micah were contemporaries and both were based in Judah. Micah was a countryman, whereas Isaiah was a townsman who ministered in the city of Jerusalem. Each had their disciples who carefully recorded and preserved their sayings. This vision of the last days has been credited to each of the prophets, but it really does not matter who originally received it. Clearly it was affirmed by the other, which gives it great authority and significance.

This is the only major prophecy to appear twice in different prophetic books. In allowing this to appear twice in the Bible it may be that God wishes to emphasise the important role that Israel will play in the last days. Taken in the context of the many prophecies foretelling the regathering of the whole house of Israel from all nations, this vision of God drawing all nations to Jerusalem takes on a new significance. God's intention is to teach all people his ways so that they may walk in his paths.

The second half of the twentieth century was a period of

rapid and significant change which saw the map of the world redrawn. Among the most significant changes was the establishment of the State of Israel and hundreds of thousands of Jews returning to the land of their forefathers. Since 1948 Israel has hardly been out of the news and the eyes of the world have been constantly focused upon Jerusalem.

Millions of pilgrims have visited the Holy City – holy to three world religions – as this prophecy foretells. It is God's desire that all people will know him and he will reveal himself to them through those who are in a covenant relationship with him through his precious Son.

God will not abandon his intention to use Israel as a light to the Gentiles. Therefore this vision can only be fulfilled after the Jews have acknowledged Jesus as Messiah, which Paul refers to in Romans 11. Eventually, as Paul also foresaw, all nations will bow the knee and acknowledge Jesus as Lord. In the rapidly changing world in which we live today, who knows how near that day is! Only God knows the answer to that.

Prayer

Thank you, O Lord, that you have broken down the middle wall of partition between Jew and Gentile. May the 'one new man' in Christ become more of a reality in our lives. Teach me your ways, O Lord, that I may walk in the paths of righteousness throughout this day.

END-TIME PEACE

Isaiah 2: 3b-5

The law will go out from Zion, the word of the Lord from Jerusalem. He will judge between the nations and will settle disputes for many peoples. They will beat their swords into ploughshares and their spears into pruning hooks. Nation will not take up sword against nation, nor will they train for war any more. Come, O house of Jacob, let us walk in the light of the Lord.

Comment:

This is the second part of the vision of the last days that both Isaiah and Micah declared in Jerusalem. The vision began with people of all nations coming to Jerusalem to seek the way of the Lord.

In the concluding passage today, the law of God goes out from Zion and the word of the Lord from Jerusalem. It depicts a time when God will summon all the nations to appear before him and he will judge them. This will mark the end of international disputes and conflict.

The day will come when God will establish his Messianic reign on earth which will be a time of universal peace. The nations will have no further use for the weapons of war but will transform them into peaceful agricultural implements.

It is a scene that encapsulates the hope of the world – a time of peace and justice when God will establish his authority over the nations and there will be no more oppression or squabbling leading to violence and war. This beautiful apocalyptic picture comes in the middle of a number of prophecies dealing with the sins of the nations and depicting the selfishness, greed and violence of man.

The prophet was no doubt spreading before the Lord the dreadful picture of the sinfulness of mankind which he saw all around him and crying out to God to deal with the situation. The Lord not only showed him the judgment that would soon fall upon a rebellious generation, but he revealed a glimpse of his final victory over sin.

This foreshadows the work of Jesus as Messiah and God's ultimate purpose of establishing his Messianic reign when Christ will return and overcome all his enemies. What a wonderful day that will be for all who belong to the Kingdom of our God. They will rejoice greatly!

Prayer

Thank you, Father, for giving us this glimpse of your ultimate purposes. Help me to live today in the power of the victory over sin won for us through the Lord Jesus Christ. Make me one of your peacemakers, through your Son, the Prince of Peace.

THE HUMBLING OF PRIDE

Isaiah 2: 12, 17-19
**The Lord Almighty has a day in store for all the proud
and lofty, for all that is exalted (and they will be
humbled)... The arrogance of man will be brought low
and the pride of men humbled; the Lord alone will be
exalted in that day, and the idols will totally disappear.
Men will flee to the caves in the rocks and to holes in the
ground from the dread of the Lord and the splendour of
his majesty, when he rises to shake the earth.**

Comment:

The words, 'The Lord Almighty has a day', form a
phrase that is regularly used by the prophets to refer to
a day of judgment. It is usually apocalyptic and part of an
end-times scenario in which God intervenes in the course
of human history to judge the nations.

Isaiah was writing in a time of considerable prosperity
when the people of Israel had become immersed in
material wealth. 'Their land is full of silver and gold; there
is no end to their treasures' (2: 7). This was the prophet's
description of the social and economic condition of the
people, but spiritually they were 'full of superstitions from
the East' (2: 6). His complaint was, 'Their land is full of
idols; they bow down to the work of their hands' (2: 8).

The prophet sees this as a grave offence against God. It
put man in the place of God. Material prosperity caused
the people to forget God and to worship the things made
by their own hands. The result of all this was an attitude of
arrogance among the people. They were proud of their
achievements. They valued their culture and elegant life-
styles. Their wealth and possessions enabled them to live in

great comfort. They felt totally secure in what they themselves had accomplished, but there was no room for God in their lives. They thought they had no need of him.

Isaiah foresaw a day when all the proud and lofty who had been exalting themselves would be humbled. He saw pride as the great stumbling-block to spiritual union with God. The pride of men had to be humbled so that God could take his rightful place; so that 'the Lord alone will be exalted' (2: 11, 17). The people who had felt secure in their material comfort will be full of dread when God shakes the earth and appears in the 'splendour of his majesty' (2: 10, 19, 21).

Isaiah's description of the 'day of the Lord' is echoed in many other prophecies such as Haggai 2: 6-7 where it is said that God will shake the nations and the whole of nature – a prophecy which is repeated in Hebrews 12: 26f.

It is all too easy to allow our material comforts to shut God out of our lives. The day will come when God will shake all the nations and the whole natural environment. Indeed, there are many signs that this is already happening; but we should not wait for such a shaking in our own lives before humbling ourselves before God and asking him to deal with our pride, so that he alone is exalted.

Prayer

Lord, make me aware of the sin of pride so that you may be exalted in my life.

WARNING SIGNS

Isaiah 3: 1a, 4, 5, 8-9
See now, the Lord, the Lord Almighty, is about to take from Jerusalem and Judah both supply and support. I will make boys their officials; mere children will govern them. People will oppress each other – man against man, neighbour against neighbour. The young will rise up against the old, the base against the honourable. Jerusalem staggers, Judah is falling; their words and deeds are against the Lord, defying his glorious presence. The look on their faces testifies against them; they parade their sin like Sodom; they do not hide it. Woe to them! They have brought disaster upon themselves.

Comment:

Isaiah was foreseeing the time when God would allow disaster to come upon the people of Jerusalem – a disaster they were bringing upon themselves. The affluence of the nation during the reign of King Uzziah, which continued under his son Jotham, would lead to the national tragedy, foreseen by the prophet, in the time of his grandson Ahaz.

The careless ease of the nation had produced a generation unresponsive to the warnings of the prophets. Micah, who was a contemporary of Isaiah, gives a vivid picture of the commercial life of the nation in the time of Jotham: the merchants cheating in the markets with dishonest scales and 'a bag of false weights', the violence and oppression among the rich and the lies and deceit among the ordinary people (Micah 6: 9-13).

Jotham's reign only lasted five years and his untimely death brought his immature, inexperienced and childish son Ahaz to the throne. His accession fulfilled the prophecy, 'I will make boys their officials; mere children will govern them'. Ahaz surrounded himself with selfish, indolent young men like himself with the inevitable result that Judah went from bad to worse. In desperation Ahaz turned to the gods of Damascus and set up their idols in the streets of Jerusalem. He even closed the Temple (2 Chronicles 28) which brought judgment upon himself and his generation.

God does not willingly send calamity upon his children. Usually we bring it upon ourselves by disregarding the warning signs he sends us and by our wilful disregard of his word. When God sends a warning or a rebuke it is always in the context of his love and mercy, coupled with his willingness to forgive and to restore us to a right relationship with himself.

Prayer

Father, reveal to me my hidden faults. Do not let me deceive myself by ignoring your loving warnings when things are wrong in my life. Open my eyes to see myself as you see me. But also make me aware of your forgiving love that I may never be afraid to confess my faults.

WASHING AWAY THE DIRT

Isaiah 4: 2-4

**In that day the Branch of the Lord will be beautiful and
glorious, and the fruit of the land will be the pride and
glory of the survivors in Israel. Those who are left in
Zion, who remain in Jerusalem, will be called holy, all
who are recorded among the living in Jerusalem. The
Lord will wash away the filth of the women of Zion; he
will cleanse the bloodstains from Jerusalem by a spirit of
judgment and a spirit of fire.**

Comment:

Liberal scholars assign this prophecy to a late date (post-
exilic) on the grounds that it reflects the thinking of a
later generation, but this is not sufficient reason to
challenge the traditional interpretation that it comes from
the early days of Isaiah's ministry. Isaiah was a prophet
with extraordinary insight. His faith in God is
demonstrated in the complete confidence with which he
predicted the downfall of Sennacherib and the failure of the
Assyrian attack upon Jerusalem (Isaiah 37: 5-7).

This confidence was rooted in his prayer life. We read in
2 Chronicles 32: 20-21a that 'King Hezekiah and the
prophet Isaiah son of Amoz cried out in prayer to heaven
about this. And the Lord sent an angel, who annihilated all
the fighting men and the leaders and officers in the camp of
the Assyrian king.' But Isaiah also foresaw that the
protection of Jerusalem would not last for ever. He told
Hezekiah, 'The time will surely come when everything in
your palace, and all that your fathers have stored up until
this day, will be carried off to Babylon' (Isaiah 39: 6).

Isaiah's recognition that destruction would eventually

come upon Jerusalem was borne out of his understanding of the holiness of God and God's requirement of righteousness among his people. Only God could cleanse the nation from its sins.

The corruption and blood guilt of the men and the complacency of the women were a deep offence to God. Judgment was inevitable; not because God *wanted* to inflict punishment upon his people whom he loved, but because he could not defend an unholy people.

The time would come when God would take away his hand of protection and allow judgment and fire to come upon the city through the onslaught of their enemies. But a remnant would survive who would be cleansed and purified by suffering and who, in repentance, would turn to the Lord.

When we deliberately shut God out of our lives we bring disaster upon ourselves. It is not the will of the Father that this should happen, but he waits for us to come to the realisation of why things have gone wrong for us. Then he can step into the situation and rebuild our lives through his great love and compassion. He washes away the dirt and the stains left upon us. As he cleanses, so he heals and restores us, filling us again with the joy of his salvation.

Prayer

We thank you, Father, that you so loved us that you sent the Lord Jesus to cleanse us from our sins and enable us to come into a right relationship with you. Help me to conduct myself in a manner more worthy of your great love.

A CANOPY OF LOVE

Isaiah 4: 5-6
Then the Lord will create over all of Mount Zion and over those who assemble there a cloud of smoke by day and a glow of flaming fire by night; over all the glory will be a canopy. It will be a shelter and shade from the heat of the day, and a refuge and hiding-place from the storm and rain.

Comment:

This is the continuation of the prophecy we were looking at yesterday. Isaiah foresaw a cleansed remnant of those who survived the catastrophe of enemy destruction in Jerusalem and Judea. He saw that the suffering which would come upon the people would bring cleansing as well as judgment. It would open the way for a mighty renewing move of God. He saw God's presence being restored to the newly liberated city.

Ezekiel foresaw in a vision the glory of God departing from Jerusalem. In this prophecy Isaiah sees the glory of God returning to Mount Zion. His presence would be signalled by a cloud of smoke by day and a glow of flaming fire by night.

This is reminiscent of the days in the wilderness during the time of Moses when God led the people with a sign of his presence. Exodus 13: 21 reports, 'By day the Lord went ahead of them in a pillar of cloud to guide them on their way and by night in a pillar of fire to give them light'.

In the vision Isaiah was given he saw an additional canopy which would provide shade from excessive heat and also shelter from storms. This canopy was a sign of God's love and protection. It is reminiscent of the banquet in the Song of Songs where the beloved one is taken into the banquet hall and rejoices that God's 'banner over me is love' (2: 4).

Isaiah saw God's canopy of protection returning over the city of Jerusalem in the time of restoration. It had only been removed because of the wilful disobedience of the people. Now, at the first sign of their repentance and turning to him, God would hasten to cover them again with the canopy of his love.

This is the way God always works in our lives. He hastens to our side, as did the father in the story Jesus told of the prodigal son's homecoming. The moment we turn to him he puts his arms of love around us, a robe of righteousness upon our shoulders, and he puts a canopy of protection over our head.

Prayer

Once again, Father, I want to thank you for your great love so freely given. Thank you for the assurance that your canopy of love will be over me throughout this day.

THE PARABLE OF THE VINEYARD

Isaiah 5: 1-2
**I will sing for the one I love a song about his vineyard:
My loved one had a vineyard on a fertile hillside. He dug
it up and cleared it of stones and planted it with the
choicest vines. He built a watchtower in it and cut out a
winepress as well. Then he looked for a crop of good
grapes, but it yielded only bad fruit.**

Comment:

The first seven verses of Isaiah 5 are the so-called 'Song
of the Vineyard' which is one of the poetic masterpieces
of the Old Testament. These two verses describe the 'plot'
of the parable. In order to understand its impact a little
imagination is required.

The scene is a busy street-market or square in the old
city of Jerusalem. In the midst of the hustle and hubbub of
trade and gossip, a singer stands on a doorstep and
announces a new song. He declares it to be of special
importance. There is something strangely compelling about
this prophetic figure that soon attracts a curious crowd of
bystanders. There is already a haunting melody in the
music he is playing even before he begins to sing.

The words grip the crowd who shuffle closer as others
press in behind. Some of them are peasant farmers used to
tending a vineyard but all of them are familiar with the
kind of scene described. The story is unfolded describing a
fertile hillside cleared of large stones; they are brought
together to form a wall around the vineyard.

The soil is carefully prepared and the best vines planted.
A wine vat has been dug in the rocky ground where the
grapes are to be trodden and the juice could run along

channels into the storage containers.

Everything possible was done to ensure a good harvest. But when the time came for the vines to produce their crop only small hard sour grapes were harvested that set the teeth on edge and were completely useless.

How often do our lives appear so 'full of promise' and yet we do not produce good fruit? How often do we let down those who look to us expectantly? How often is God disappointed with us?

We know we have a Father in heaven who understands our infirmities and who loves and forgives us despite our failings. Those who first heard this song did not yet know the full extent of the forgiving grace of God or his redeeming love that was one day to be revealed through Jesus the Messiah. When we truly know him our lives should reflect the love of God. The good fruit of the Holy Spirit should be there for all to see.

Prayer

Father, we are so grateful that we are able to know you through Jesus our Lord and Saviour. We confess our unworthiness and we praise you for your forgiving grace and renewing love. Please give to us your Holy Spirit, that we may produce good fruit in our lives.

WHAT MORE COULD I DO?

Isaiah 5: 3-4
'Now you dwellers in Jerusalem and men of Judah, judge between me and my vineyard. What more could have been done for my vineyard than I have done for it? When I looked for good grapes, why did it yield only bad?'

Comment:

Having set forth the parable in the first two verses the prophet/singer now appeals to his hearers. The story he began was about a vineyard owned by a friend, one whom he loved, but the song now takes a new turn with the storyteller fading into the background. Suddenly the owner of the vineyard makes a direct appeal.

The audience is addressed formally as 'dwellers in Jerusalem and men of Judah'. But they are not asked to offer advice as to what has gone wrong. The appeal to them is twofold. First, to act as witnesses; secondly, to give judgment.

The audience is invited to bear witness that the owner has done everything possible to ensure a good crop of grapes. Had he not lavished every care upon the vineyard? Surely there was nothing more that he could have done?

The audience then has to make a decision. They are invited to be judge between the owner and his vineyard. Why was it that when he had done everything possible to ensure a good harvest it yielded only bad fruit?

At this stage of the parable the audience still did not realise that they were being set up to act as judge and jury in their own case. God's complaint against his people was that he had lavished upon them every kind of care and blessing. Additionally he had revealed all that needed to be known concerning his own nature and purposes.

The word of God had been conveyed clearly to his people. Yet they were slow to understand, rebellious in their nature. They turned away from the paths of righteousness into sin, preferring darkness to light, despite all that God had done to communicate his love and his truth.

How often does God say to us, 'What more could I have done for you than I have already done?'

This question reveals both the love of God and the sadness in the heart of God that his children can be so unresponsive.

How many parents of rebellious children have asked, 'What more could I have done for you?' If we as human parents can grieve over loved ones who are ungrateful, can we not understand the grief of God? It may be that this word is addressed to you. 'What more could I have done for you than I have already done?'

Prayer

Father, I acknowledge that you have lavished your love and your blessings upon me throughout my life. Forgive me for the many times I have missed opportunities to serve you and have produced only bad fruit.

WHAT WILL I DO?

Isaiah 5: 5-6

'Now I will tell you what I am going to do to my vineyard: I will take away its hedge, and it will be destroyed; I will break down its wall, and it will be trampled. I will make it a wasteland, neither pruned nor cultivated, and briers and thorns will grow there. I will command the clouds not to rain on it.'

Comment:

By the time the prophet/singer reached this point in the unfolding parable in his Song of the Vineyard, the audience must have been growing uncomfortably aware that this was no ordinary song. They were being involved in a drama that had far greater significance than the mere failure of the grape harvest.

The song ceased appealing to them to act as judge and jury – suddenly the owner of the vineyard himself pronounced judgment: 'I will tell you what I am going to do with my vineyard'.

The vineyard, over which so much care and protection had been given, suddenly saw its hedge taken away. It was thus exposed to strong winds that would blow away the blossom and even the first signs of fruit.

Next the wall was broken down leaving it exposed to the attacks of wild animals. The cultivated land was neglected; the weeds were not removed, neither were the branches pruned. Wild thorns and thistles grew up on the land and choked the vines.

By this time the people listening to the song must have become aware that the parable was directed against them. The uncultivated land covered in briers was a familiar sight in areas that had been plundered by an enemy and stripped of its inhabitants. The threat implied in the parable was becoming inescapable.

Suddenly there was no doubt. The word 'command' rang through the air, stunning the listeners. The vineyard owner was none other than the Lord God Almighty for he alone had the ability to say, 'I will *command* the clouds not to rain on it'. The audience could do no more than wait sullenly for the final pronouncement of the parable at which we look tomorrow.

The lesson for us as individuals as well as for the nations is that God's blessings are always conditional. His love is unconditional; but his blessings are conditional upon our response to his word. He looks for a response of love, and righteous living.

Does God see good fruit in the nation? Does he see good fruit in his church? Perhaps the most important question is, does he see good fruit in the individual lives of his people, those who acknowledge Jesus as their Lord and Saviour?

Prayer
Father, help me to see myself as you see me. Forgive me for the many times I am unresponsive to your word.

THE VERDICT

Isaiah 5: 7

The vineyard of the Lord Almighty is the house of Israel, and the men of Judah are the garden of his delight. And he looked for justice, but saw bloodshed; for righteousness, but heard cries of distress.

Comment:

This verse concludes the parable of the vineyard. The prophet/singer abruptly changes from the almost plaintive song with which he began to a tone of unyielding accusation. In a few terse lines he unveils the whole purpose of the parable. 'The vineyard of the Lord Almighty is the house of Israel, and the men of Judah are the garden of his delight.' Judah and Israel are the twin nations from the stock of Abraham whom God had, centuries ago, drawn into a covenant relationship with himself. He had watched over them, nurtured and protected them, yet they had spurned his love.

Israel and Judah had broken their covenant relationship with God. He had given them clear direction and they had freely entered into solemn promises of faithfulness to God and obedience to his word. But they had forsaken his commands and turned away from him. 'He looked for justice, but saw bloodshed; for righteousness, but heard cries of distress.'

God's patience is amazing, his love is beyond measure, but our wilful rebellion exposes us to the enemy and disaster overtakes us when we refuse to heed his warnings. This pronouncement upon an unjust and unrighteous generation of rebellious people paved the way for the seven woes that follow in this chapter, and in Chapter 10.

Those who know the requirements of God condemn themselves if they do not follow them. We cannot claim that God is unjust if we know his word and we have deliberately turned our backs upon it. God is then fully justified if he withdraws his hand of protection from over our lives and allows us to go our own way, even though it means our lives are exposed to all kinds of evil influences that eventually bring disaster upon us. But this is not God's desire.

Time after time God sends warning signs to us which are coupled with the Father's plea to return to him so that he can put a robe of righteousness upon us and enfold us within his arms of love and protection.

Prayer

Overcome my stubbornness, O Lord. Help me to hear and to heed your warnings and to respond to your love. Keep your protection around me and around those I love.

THE SEVEN WOES

Isaiah 5: 8-10

Woe to you who add house to house and join field to field till no space is left and you live alone in the land. The Lord Almighty has declared in my hearing: 'Surely the great houses will become desolate, the fine mansions left without occupants. A ten-acre vineyard will produce only a bath of wine, a homer of seed only an ephah of grain.'

Comment:

This is the first of the seven woes that Isaiah brings following the Song of the Vineyard. This one should really be headed 'Woe to the Greedy'. It is directed squarely towards the rich who have been using their wealth to purchase land and property thus depriving the poor of any chance of making a satisfactory living.

The rich landlords were buying up the houses of the poor as they got into debt and taking the fields of peasant farmers who were unfortunate enough to owe them money. Small independent farmers were losing land that had been in their family for generations and now simply served to enhance the estates of wealthy landowners.

The prophet saw the injustice of the situation as intolerable in the eyes of the Lord Almighty who is a God of justice. God had instituted the Jubilee for the protection of small farmers, so that on the fiftieth year land would be restored to its original owner. But these regulations were being ignored and the poor were being cheated out of their inheritance.

Judgment had already been declared in the hearing of the prophet. The fate of the rich oppressors had already been sealed in the council of the Lord – 'The great houses will become desolate, the fine mansions left without occupants'.

Unless the warning was heeded, God would withdraw his hand of protection from over the nation because it was steeped in injustice, which was an intolerable offence to a God of justice. He would allow their enemies to sweep across the land destroying the great houses of the wealthy.

As if this were not enough, God himself would bring judgment upon the unjust nation by reducing their harvests, probably by withholding the spring rains so that fields and vineyards would not produce sufficient to feed the nation.

We ignore God's warnings at our peril. We really cannot get away with injustice. But injustice and oppression are not simply the prerogative of the wealthy. Even the poor often oppress each other, within the family, or in marriage, or at work, or within the local community. Any misuse of our position of authority, or even of the power we have over others because of their love for us, becomes an offence in the eyes of a just and loving God.

Prayer

Lord, make me sensitive to injustice. Alert your people to those things which are an offence to you. Bring justice to the nations.

THE JUSTICE OF GOD

Isaiah 5: 11-17

Woe to those who rise early in the morning to run after their drinks... but they have no regard for the deeds of the Lord, no respect for the work of his hands. Therefore my people will go into exile for lack of understanding... Therefore the grave enlarges its appetite and opens its mouth without limit... so man will be brought low and mankind humbled... But the Lord Almighty will be exalted by his justice, and the holy God will show himself holy by his righteousness.

Comment:

This is the second of the seven woes and it is directed, not only towards the ruling classes, but to all who are 'brawlers and revellers', both 'nobles and masses' (v 14). This passage reflects a careless, irresponsible society indulging in the excesses of luxury, while giving no thought to the consequences.

The prophet describes a scene of drunkenness and dissolute living in which the rulers begin drinking early in the morning so that their minds are inflamed with alcohol and they are therefore unable to think clearly. It shows the whole society as indulging in banquets and living in a way that pays no regard to the consequences of their actions. He says that they have 'no regard for the deeds of the Lord'.

Prophecy is rooted in the consistency of God. He was not capricious like the gods of the pagans who worshipped idols, whose nature could never be known, and whose response to supplication could never be forecast. God had revealed his nature and purposes. He was known personally by his prophets who regularly stood in his council and declared his word to the nation.

There was no excuse for 'lack of understanding'. God would allow the nation to go into exile because they wilfully disregarded the warning signs he sent to them. In fact, when God did allow the enemies of Israel and Judah to triumph over them, this would actually be a demonstration of his own justice! 'The holy God will show himself holy by his righteousness' in refusing to defend an unrighteous people.

We cannot blame God when everything goes wrong in the life of the nation or in our personal lives if we have wilfully disregarded the warning signs that God, in his love and mercy, sends to us. Wealth and social prestige cannot save us – 'Both low and high will be humbled' unless they return to the Lord and heed his words.

Prayer

Father, we acknowledge that we are part of a sinful nation whose people do not seek your way or listen to your word. Raise up your church to declare your word in the nation. Strengthen my own witness in my family and among my friends.

THE CURE FOR DECEIT

Isaiah 5: 18-19

Woe to those who draw sin along with cords of deceit, and wickedness as with cart ropes, to those who say, 'Let God hurry, let him hasten his work so that we may see it. Let it approach, let the plan of the Holy One of Israel come, so that we may know it.'

Comment:

In this third woe the prophet concentrates upon deceitfulness. He sees it dragging the nation towards disaster like the ropes that harness the oxen to a cart. The cart is powerless to determine the direction in which it is pulled by the straining ropes. Both the rulers of the nation and the masses are so thoroughly deceived that they are oblivious to the consequences of what is happening around them and the consequences of their rebellion against God.

Deceitfulness had reached such a point in the life of the nation that the people were actually blaspheming against God without even realising it. They were saying, 'Let God hurry!' If he really does have good plans for Israel let him demonstrate his goodness by doing something quickly to bless the nation. They were saying, 'Why doesn't God hurry up and get on with his work so that everyone can see it, then we will believe in the goodness of God?'

This was similar to the kind of challenge that was hurled at Jesus by unbelievers at the time of the Crucifixion. Those who passed by shook their heads and said, 'Come down from the cross, if you are the Son of God!' (Matthew 27: 40).

Unbelief causes us to have a hardness of heart towards God so that we are driven by deceit or pulled helplessly along like the ox cart in this prophecy. The baser side of our nature becomes dominant. As Jeremiah observed, the human heart 'is deceitful above all things and beyond cure' (17: 9).

Paul gave the answer that is at the heart of the gospel. It was because we are helpless to stand up against the deceit that is endemic to our nature that God sent his own Son, our Saviour, Jesus.

Through Christ we can be reconciled with God; we are brought into a right relationship with him and experience in our lives a freedom from deceit and a peace that passes all understanding. Paul says that in Christ we are able to discard the 'old self which is being corrupted by its deceitful desires' and we are then able 'to put on the new self, created to be like God in true righteousness and holiness' (Ephesians 4: 22-24).

Prayer

Lord, we confess that we are often guilty of self-deception. We acknowledge that you alone can truly heal the heart. Help me to walk in truth and holiness.

REVERSING VALUES

Isaiah 5: 20
**Woe to those who call evil good and good evil, who put
darkness for light and light for darkness, who put bitter
for sweet and sweet for bitter.**

Comment:

In this fourth woe the prophet describes tersely the way in
which basic social and spiritual values are being turned
upside-down in his day. The deceitfulness that is gripping
the nation has progressed to such a degree that it has
actually turned upside down the basic morality upon
which the health and stability of the nation depends.

Once that moral and spiritual foundation crumbles and
disappears the whole life of the nation is threatened. A
society cannot survive without shared values that are
commonly accepted, such as truth, honesty and integrity. If
lying is acceptable and promises are worthless, then
stability in social life and commerce becomes impossible.

In Isaiah's time he saw a nation that was actually so
corrupt that everyone adjusted the rules of social behaviour
to suit their individual needs and enable them to pursue
their own selfish ambitions regardless of the cost to others.
They actually called good evil and evil good.

In our own generation we are seeing this happen in a
more polite and subtle way whereby we obscure sin by
changing the name to make it sound nice, acceptable
behaviour. For example:

We speak of people being 'gay', which obscures the fact
that they are practising sodomy, which the Bible says is
detestable in God's eyes.

We speak of people 'sleeping together', which hides the fact that they are engaging in fornication or adultery.

We speak of 'terminating a pregnancy' instead of murdering an unborn child

We refer to a 'foetus' instead of a baby.

We speak of 'adjusting our tax returns' to obscure the fact that we are stealing from the wealth of the nation.

We say we are going to see someone is 'all right', which means we are practising bribery.

We are pleased when someone does not charge us VAT, we pay cash with no questions asked in shady deals, which is corruption.

We boast about speeding, which is law breaking.

We use our employer's telephone or are careless about timekeeping, or pocketing sundry items, which is cheating.

We exaggerate, which is lying.

There is a multitude of ways in which our behaviour is unrighteous.

Even those engaged in the work of the gospel boast about their ministry being 'blessed', trying to show how they are favoured by God. In reality they are falling victim to the oldest tricks of the enemy. The sin of pride is so subtle! How easily we are deceived!

Prayer
Lord, hold back your servant from sin. Make me aware of unrighteousness and make me responsive to the prompting of your Holy Spirit.

WHO ARE THE WISE?

Isaiah 5: 21
Woe to those who are wise in their own eyes and clever in their own sight.

Comment:

Today we come to the fifth woe which is the shortest of the seven. It gives no explanation and no elaboration to enable us to get a picture of what the prophet had in mind. It simply consists of a bald statement of judgment upon those who, in their own eyes, are wise and clever.

For an explanation of what is in the prophet's mind we need to go to Jeremiah who says, 'This is what the Lord says: "Let not the wise man boast of his wisdom or the strong man boast of his strength or the rich man boast of his riches, but let him who boasts boast about this: that he understands and knows me, that I am the Lord, who exercises kindness, justice and righteousness on earth, for in these I delight", declares the Lord' (9: 23-24).

The prophets knew that true wisdom is only to be found in God. It is only those who know him who can understand the mystery of life. For until we begin to grasp something of the nature and purposes of God, our eyes are blinkered and we can only see things through a short-term worldly perspective. As we come to know God we begin to perceive the spiritual dimension of life which changes our entire perspective.

One of the commonest faults of humanity is to overrate ourselves, to count ourselves more highly than we should. Even if we don't boast about our cleverness, or our wisdom, or education, or intelligence, or sharpness of perception, it is there in the secrecy of our own minds and it affects our attitude towards others. More importantly it affects our attitude towards God. We cannot be humble before God when we are puffed up with pride.

It is time we took seriously the teaching of Paul that God has 'made foolish the wisdom of the world'. It was for this reason that Paul did not rely upon clever arguments in his preaching. Instead he said, 'My message and my preaching were not with wise and persuasive words, but with a demonstration of the Spirit's power, so that your faith might not rest on men's wisdom, but on God's power' (1 Corinthians 2: 4).

Prayer

Lord, help me not to be wise or clever in my own eyes. Forgive me for my foolish pride. Help me to have a genuine attitude of humility in your sight, O Lord.

THE CONSEQUENCE OF CORRUPTION

Isaiah 5: 22-25a

Woe to those who are heroes at drinking wine and champions at mixing drinks, who acquit the guilty for a bribe, but deny justice to the innocent. Therefore, as tongues of fire lick up straw and as dry grass sinks down in the flames, so their roots will decay and their flowers blow away like dust, for they have rejected the law of the Lord Almighty and spurned the word of the Holy One of Israel. Therefore the Lord's anger burns against his people.

Comment:

This sixth woe is directed against the lawlessness of the nations. There is corruption among the judges who accept bribery and give judgment in favour of the rich, thus oppressing the poor with a complete disregard for justice. The prophet sees the root cause of the problems in the nation as being due to the fact that they have 'rejected the law of the Almighty and spurned the word of the Holy One of Israel'.

Isaiah's message was that, because of this rejection of the word of God, disaster would come upon the nation. It would not simply be the enemies of Israel who would strike them down but the hand of the Lord would actually be raised against his own people: 'his hand is raised and he strikes them down' (v 25). In the vision the prophet sees dead bodies lying like refuse in the streets (v 25).

The consequences of deliberately turning away from God and rejecting his word are always terrible whether it is in the life of the nation or that of individuals. Once we have known God we have no excuse. We cannot claim ignorance or pretend to be innocent.

God knows our hearts, and although we may deceive ourselves or even deceive others, we cannot deceive God. Once we spurn the word of God we allow corruption to enter and, like rust spreading through iron, it gains an increasing hold until the whole framework is affected and there is no substance left.

If it were not for the mercy of God there would be no hope for anyone, but God has actually provided for the sinfulness and corruption in our human nature. As Paul declares, 'If anyone is in Christ, he is a new creation; the old has gone, the new has come! All this is from God, who reconciled us to himself through Christ' (2 Corinthians 5: 17-18). The new life in Christ is available to us today. We don't have to wait! We only have to ask him for it.

Even when we are believers we can become corrupted by the world. Our spiritual life becomes dry. We no longer bear good fruit. It is time to seek the Lord for a fresh experience of his Holy Spirit.

Prayer

Lord, you know my true spiritual condition. I cannot deceive you. Cleanse me; renew a right spirit within me and restore to me today the joy of your salvation.

ISAIAH'S COMMISSION

Isaiah 6: 1-2

In the year that King Uzziah died, I saw the Lord seated on a throne, high and exalted, and the train of his robe filled the temple. Above him were seraphs, each with six wings. With two wings they covered their faces, with two they covered their feet, and with two they were flying.

Comment:

Isaiah was probably at prayer or worshipping in the Temple when he received an unforgettable experience of the presence of the Lord. The ornately carved seraphim high up in the dome of the Temple were no doubt a familiar sight to him but on this occasion their physical reality became blurred and lost in the blinding reality of the presence of the living God. He appeared enthroned and exalted so that, to the young Isaiah, it seemed that his majesty filled the whole Temple.

It was a significant moment in the life of the young man who was to become one of Israel's greatest prophets. But it was also a significant time in the life of the nation. King Uzziah had just died after a long reign of 52 years. It was the end of an era. The whole nation recognised that it was a time of great change.

King Uzziah had been a leper for a number of years. He was an outcast from the nation, banned from the Temple. The whole nation had been feeling unclean, as though a curse from the Lord had descended upon all the people. The gloom of this period was not lifted until the death of Uzziah. Now there was hope that a new era had dawned. It was with this hope in mind that the young Isaiah was worshipping in the Temple when he experienced the call of the Lord to be his prophet. This was a turning point in the life of the nation. The word of the Lord would once again be heard with power and clarity.

How often God has to allow us to go through a time of deep despair before we are ready to hear and to receive his word! But when the new day dawns the gloom of darkness is banished in the glorious light of his presence.

This is always the experience of the Lord's people. Even in the darkest times when we go through difficult days, or days of great suffering, he is with us. His presence slowly transforms the darkness into light as we allow him to take control even of our emotions. He lifts the gloom and radiates new hope filling us with his love and joy. It all seems impossible at the time, but as we relax in his presence, it actually happens!

Prayer

Lord, you know those areas of my life that need your transforming, life-giving touch. Help me to receive what you are longing to give.

THE HOLINESS OF GOD

Isaiah 6: 3-5

They were calling to one another: 'Holy, holy, holy is the Lord Almighty; the whole earth is full of his glory.' At the sound of their voices the doorposts and thresholds shook and the temple was filled with smoke. 'Woe to me!' I cried. 'I am ruined! For I am a man of unclean lips, and I live among a people of unclean lips, and my eyes have seen the King, the Lord Almighty.'

Comment:

Isaiah's reaction to his experience of the presence of God was an overwhelming sense of awe. In the vision he heard the seraphim calling to one another 'Holy, holy, holy is the Lord Almighty'. It was this sense of the holiness of God and the awesome reality that he, a mere mortal, had been privileged to be allowed into the presence of the living God that stirred the young prophet to the depths of his spiritual being.

The experience of the holiness of God reminded Isaiah of his own creatureliness. Who was he, a mere created man, to enter the presence of the Almighty? No doubt there flooded into his mind at the same moment the corrupt state of the nation that for years had basked in the complacency of prosperity yet whose king had been a leper and an outcast, not even able to worship with his people. The ceremonially unclean king seemed to symbolise the uncleanness of the nation.

With his sensitive nature, the young prophet immediately associated himself with the sinfulness of his generation. He, too, was a man of unclean lips who lived among a people of unclean lips. Yet with his own eyes he had been permitted to see the true King of the nation, the Lord Almighty, the Holy One of Israel. How could he survive such an experience? Surely his uncleanness would pronounce a sentence of death upon him, but for the mercy of God!

O that our generation today, that fears neither God nor man, would have a greater sense of awe before the Lord Almighty, Creator of the Universe! We are so surrounded by works of concrete and brick, the creations of man, that we rarely stand with the Psalmist to gaze up into the heavens and experience the presence of the living God (Psalm 27: 4).

Our spiritual lives would benefit if we would stand aside from the ordinary pursuits of our daily lives and enter into the majestic presence of the God who set the stars in their orbits, and say within ourselves, 'What is man that thou art mindful of him?' (Psalm 8: 4, AV).

Perhaps the most needful spiritual experience, not only among secular man, but also among believers today, is a sense of awe such as Isaiah experienced in the presence of the holy God whose glory fills the whole earth.

Prayer
Holy, holy, holy, are you, O Lord Almighty. The whole earth is full of your glory. What am I that you should care for me? Yet I know that you do!

THE ATONEMENT

Isaiah 6: 6-7

Then one of the seraphs flew to me with a live coal in his hand, which he had taken with tongs from the altar. With it he touched my mouth and said, 'See, this has touched your lips; your guilt is taken away and your sin atoned for'.

Comment:

Isaiah's experience of the holiness of God and his own uncleanness was followed immediately by the experience of God's cleansing hand upon his life. This experience expresses the heart of our faith: the very moment we humble ourselves before God, he acts to restore us to himself.

God never cuts us off from fellowship with himself. It is sin that severs the relationship with the Father. Like the Prodigal Son, the moment we come to ourselves, to a recognition of our pitiful condition, God acts to restore us to a right relationship with himself. God does this through atoning for our sin. This atonement brings about our 'at-one-ment' with the Father.

It should not surprise us that Isaiah experienced God's act of atonement more than 700 years before Calvary. Atonement for sin is a central theme of the Hebrew scriptures as well as the New Testament. This underlines the consistency of God, who revealed to his prophet that salvation lies at the very heart of his purposes for mankind, and that this can only be achieved through an act of God himself.

Isaiah's realisation of his own sinfulness and his cry to the Lord, prepared the way for the revelation he received of

God's act of atonement, whereby he takes away the offence of the penitent sinner. Not only did Isaiah experience the forgiveness of sin but he was also given assurance that his guilt had been taken away.

It is this assurance that brings what Paul described as 'the peace which passes all understanding' (Philippians 4: 7). This amazing peace comes into the life of each believer who experiences the love and forgiveness of the Father who so loved the world that he gave his only begotten Son and allowed him to die upon a cross for the atonement of our sin. 'He has appeared once for all at the end of the ages to do away with sin by the sacrifice of himself' (Hebrews 9: 26).

Through Christ we find our 'at-one-ment' with the Father and the assurance that we can rest secure in his love. Such an assurance fills us with a deep peace that the world cannot give, neither can it understand.

Prayer

Thank you Father for sending your precious Son, the Lord Jesus; for taking away my sin and removing all guilt. Increase in me the experience of being at one with you throughout this day.

RESPONDING TO GOD

Isaiah 6: 8-9

Then I heard the voice of the Lord saying, 'Whom shall I send? And who will go for us?' And I said, 'Here am I. Send me!'

Comment:

Isaiah's experience of being brought into a right relationship with God was followed immediately by his call. With no hesitation the young prophet responded. His response was followed immediately by the experience of being commissioned by God as a prophet to the nation.

God does not waste time. He had appeared to the young Isaiah for a purpose. God's hand was already upon his life. He had formed him in his mother's womb and watched over him and nurtured him to bring him to this point where he was ready to experience the presence and the holiness of the Lord Almighty.

This experience of God having watched over his life from birth is referred to in Isaiah 49: 1 – 'Before I was born the Lord called me; from my birth he made mention of my name'. Both Jeremiah (1: 5) and David (Psalm 139: 13) gave a similar testimony. God watches over us from the moment of conception until he takes us home to be with him.

Isaiah's immediate response to the call of God reflected his new-found spiritual experience. This was not grounded in a confidence of the flesh, or in any sense of his own worthiness. His confidence was solely in the Lord who had transformed his sense of unworthiness. He had done this by taking away his sin and even removing from him the crippling experience of guilt, thus leaving him free to serve the Lord with a pure heart.

Isaiah had the faith to know that if God called him to do a task, he would supply all the necessary resources. If God called him to a ministry, however difficult it proved to be, he would give the enabling for that ministry. The prophet was therefore able to respond with confidence in the faithfulness of the Lord.

Once we have this confidence in what God has done for us we too can respond, 'Here am I. Send me!'

God wants to use your life in a unique way. He knows the gifts he has given you and he knows the circumstances of your life. There are things that only you can do. His call to you today is, 'Whom shall I send? Who will go for us?' God is longing to hear your eager response, 'Here am I, send me!'

Prayer

Lord, I hear your call to serve you. 'Here I am. Send me! Please equip me, fill me, embolden me and guide me, for the honour of your holy name.

SPIRITUAL BLINDNESS

Isaiah 6: 9-10
He said, 'Go and tell this people: "You will be ever hearing, but never understanding; you will be ever seeing, but never perceiving. This people's heart has become calloused, they hardly hear with their ears, and they have closed their eyes. Otherwise they might see with their eyes, hear with their ears, understand with their hearts, and turn and be healed."' (Septuagint. NIV margin)

Comment:

There is a significant difference in this passage between the Hebrew and the Greek texts. The Hebrew uses an imperative which implies that God instructed the prophet to harden the hearts of the people so that they would not be saved.

The difference between the Hebrew and the Greek text highlights the contrast between the 'active' and the 'passive' out-working of the will of God: ie, the things God initiates and those that he simply allows to happen. For the prophets, this was not a problem. It was merely two different ways of expressing the same thing. But for our western minds it is abhorrent to think that God would tell people to hear but never understand, and see but never perceive! Isaiah would have found no difficulty in giving such a message because God had already revealed to him that this was what was going to happen!

The Septuagint text shows God revealing to the prophet the difficult task he would face in declaring a message to the people which they would reject. In hardening their hearts against God's call to repentance they would refuse to turn to him and be healed. We have preferred the Septuagint text for our reading as being closer to the revelation of the nature of God in the book of Isaiah, expressed in a manner more familiar to western readers.

This first message Isaiah had to declare gave him a foretaste of the difficulties he was to face throughout his ministry. God was preparing him for the onerous task of speaking to a rebellious people who would hear with their ears but never with understanding. They would see with their eyes, but never perceive in their spirit.

The hearts of the people had become calloused by their self-will and the spirit of rebellion against God which had gripped the nation. This created a spiritual blindness which dulled their perception. Their minds were closed to the significance of events in their lifetime. They were unable to perceive the activity of God or to appreciate the warning signs he was sending them. They were even unable to hear, with understanding, the direct warnings and clear interpretation of events which Isaiah unfolded to them.

This is always the sorrow of the Father that his children are so stubborn and so slow and dull in their spiritual understanding that even the simple truth of his great love for each one of us is not understood and grasped.

There are many things that God is longing to say to you today which require your spiritual receptivity which has been dulled by worldly values. God is wanting a new openness to receive what he desires to communicate. He can only do this as your heart is softened. He alone can open your eyes and ears and give you understanding.

Prayer
Lord, give me ears to hear, eyes to see and a heart that is open to you, that I may be responsive to your word today through the ministry of your Holy Spirit in my life.

NEW GROWTH

Isaiah 6: 11 and 13
Then I said, 'For how long, O Lord?' And he answered: 'Until the cities lie ruined and without inhabitant, until the houses are left deserted and the fields ruined and ravaged. And though a tenth remains in the land, it will again be laid waste. But as the terebinth and oak leave stumps when they are cut down, so the holy seed will be the stump in the land.'

Comment:

The young Isaiah was given a vision of things that would happen many years later. The prophecy was fulfilled towards the end of his own lifetime when the Assyrian armies swept across the land leaving a trail of destruction and desolate towns and villages in their wake. The Assyrians often carried out what today would be described as a 'scorched earth policy', destroying harvests as well as houses.

At the same time as Isaiah was given this depressing picture he was also shown that the nation would not be totally destroyed, but that a remnant would survive. This revelation about a remnant was an important milestone in the development of the Hebraic understanding of the nature and purpose of God. He is not a God who depends upon large numbers. Gideon learned this lesson when God reduced his army of 32,000 to a mere 300! (Judges 7).

A small number who are prepared to put their trust totally in the Lord are far more use to him than a half-hearted multitude. Only two men out of the whole of Israel survived the forty years in the wilderness under Moses' leadership. But they were the ones whom God prepared to be the leaders of his people when they crossed the Jordan and entered the promised land (Deuteronomy 1:36).

Isaiah saw that there was hope for the future in a remnant. It was this revelation that gave him the confidence to encourage King Hezekiah to resist the demands of the Assyrians for the surrender of Jerusalem.

Isaiah knew that even though God sometimes allows his people to go through difficult times, he would bring them through to victory. These difficult times God often uses for cleansing and purifying his people. This happened many times in the history of Israel.

The Lord wants us to know today that there are no difficulties which are insurmountable. Once our lives are given into his hands he has control.

The message to each one of us is that God is faithful. If you listen quietly you will hear him reassuring you that he will never desert you. He will bring you through even the darkest hour. Those things which seem humanly impossible are possible to God. The victory is assured!

Prayer

Lord, give me eyes to see beyond the immediate, to perceive your purposes and to understand the things that perplex me. Even though I cannot see the end from the beginning, give me the confidence to trust you totally for today.

FIRM FAITH

Isaiah 7: 2-3a, 4a and 9b
Now the house of David was told, 'Aram has allied itself with Ephraim'; so the hearts of Ahaz and his people were shaken, as the trees of the forest are shaken by the wind. Then the Lord said to Isaiah, 'Go out, you and your son Shear-Jashub, to meet Ahaz... Say to him, "Be careful, keep calm and don't be afraid. Do not lose heart because of these two smouldering stubs of firewood... If you do not stand firm in your faith, you will not stand at all."'

Comment:

This was a time of change in the turbulent history of Middle East politics. The rising power of Assyria under the new emperor Tiglath Pileser threatened the independence of all the little nation-states of the West such as Edom, Moab, Syria, Lebanon, Gaza, Israel and Judah.

It seems that Syria (Aram) and Israel tried to form some kind of coalition in order to resist the threatened Assyrian invasion. They tried to persuade Judah to join them but Ahaz would have none of it. As a consequence, Syria and Israel joined forces to attack Judah and tried to force Ahaz to change his mind.

Isaiah applauded the decision not to join the coalition. He saw the kings of Syria and Israel as two bits of firewood making a lot of smoke but from whom the fire was already extinguished. They were powerless to stand against the purposes of God. He counselled Ahaz to stand firm and to put his faith in God alone. But Ahaz was not a man of faith and everything he did turned to disaster.

The combined army of Israel and Syria attacked Judah with such force that, in one day, they killed 120,000 of

Judah's soldiers (2 Chronicles 28: 6). This made Ahaz all the more uncertain of his faith and in desperation he began worshipping the gods of Damascus. The account in 2 Chronicles 28: 23 says that 'he thought, "Since the gods of the kings of Aram have helped them, I will sacrifice to them so that they will help me." But they were his downfall and the downfall of all Israel.'

'If you do not stand firm in your faith, you will not stand at all' (v 9b). This was the message of Isaiah to Ahaz and it is the message God wants his people to hear today.

Whatever circumstances you are facing, know that God can change even the most impossible situations. But even if, in his sovereign and perfect will, he chooses not to act in the way you expect or would wish, what he desires is faith.

The Hebrew word for faith, *emunah*, has much to do with faithfulness. Faith is believing that God is reliable; it is faithfully trusting him, no matter what befalls us; it is standing firm to the end. God always honours such faith and blesses his faithful ones.

Prayer

Lord I believe, help me in my unbelief. Renew my confidence in you, O Lord, and give me the strength to take that leap of faith from which fear so often holds me back.

GOD WITH US

Isaiah 7: 13-14, 16

Then Isaiah said, 'Hear now, you house of David! Is it not enough to try the patience of men? Will you try the patience of my God also? Therefore the Lord himself will give you a sign: The virgin will be with child and will give birth to a son, and will call him Immanuel... But before the boy knows enough to reject the wrong and choose the right, the land of the two kings you dread will be laid waste.'

Comment:

Although Isaiah was pleased when King Ahaz refused to join a confederation of nations against Assyria, he was appalled when Ahaz sent envoys to Nineveh asking the Assyrians for help. The assistance he was seeking was against his brothers in Israel who had joined Syria against Judah.

Isaiah's counsel had been for the king and the nation to put their trust in the Lord, not to call for help from a pagan emperor. He said that in the time it takes for a young maiden to conceive and bear a child and for the child to reach the first stages of infant understanding – in just such a short time – the kings of Syria and Israel, who were presently threatening Judah, would be swept aside.

Isaiah was concerned with the long-term implications of making an alliance with Assyria. He correctly foresaw that the rising power of Assyria would soon sweep across to the Mediterranean Sea conquering all the small nations in their path.

In addition to foreseeing the downfall of Israel and Syria, Isaiah also foresaw the time coming when Assyria would attack Judah. He therefore urged Ahaz to seek a sign from God. The King refused, so the prophet brought the word that forms our reading for today.

In this prophecy Isaiah was evidently seeing something of greater significance than the contemporary political situation. He saw that it was God's intention to come amongst his people, being born among them as a human baby that he might dwell in their midst. He foresaw a child being born who would be called Immanuel – 'God with us'.

This prophecy has taken on new significance for believers in the Lord Jesus since his first advent. But it has always been God's desire that his presence among his people should be recognised.

That same longing is in the Father's heart today and he wants you to know that he is right here with you today. He is with you and he will never leave you. That is the meaning of one of the beautiful names given to Jesus – Immanuel.

Yet our knowledge and experience of God's closeness are dependent upon our response to him. We are to seek the Lord with all our heart. 'Come near to God and he will come near to you' (James 4: 8).

Prayer

Father, we thank you that in every generation you have never left your people alone. Open my eyes today so that I may see your presence and feel your nearness. Let me know the truth that you are right here with me and you will remain with me throughout this day. Help me to seek you with all my heart.

FEAR GOD NOT MEN

Isaiah 8: 12-14a
'Do not call for a treaty every time these people call for a treaty; do not fear what they fear, and do not dread it. The Lord Almighty is the one you are to regard as holy, he is the one you are to fear, he is the one you are to dread, and he will be a sanctuary.' (NIV margin)

Comment:

This is a difficult passage to translate and in our reading today we are following the text given in the NIV margin. The AV speaks of a 'confederacy' and the RSV and NIV use the word 'conspiracy', but 'treaty' accords better with the historical circumstances of this prophecy.

The political life of the nation was in turmoil at this time. Isaiah was appalled at the intrigues, plots and conspiracies that were going on in Jerusalem. King Ahaz was a weak, unrighteous ruler who was torn between the pro-Egypt party and the pro-Assyria party among his political advisers. He was a man with no firm foundation of faith, who was driven by expediency.

Isaiah's counsel was not to negotiate a treaty with any of the pagan nations but for the king and the people to put their trust in God. He never lost his own sense of the holiness of God that began with a powerful vision of the presence of God in the Temple at the time of his call to ministry. He urged the nation to exchange their fear of man for a fear of God.

All the prophets of Israel had a strong sense of awe in the presence of God. They knew him to be the Almighty, the God of the Universe who held the nations in his hands. Isaiah approached the political and social problems of his day from this basic standpoint. Thus he declared that Judah had nothing to fear from the hostile nations. The only thing that she should fear was stepping outside God's protection by failing to trust him. The sin of the leaders of the nation was that they were more afraid of men than of God.

Fear of God does not mean being afraid in the sense that we are afraid of wicked and violent men. Fear of God is reverence, a sense of awe in the presence of the Almighty, the Creator of the Universe who holds the destiny of kings and rulers in his hands, but who also keeps his covenant promises to his people.

Many believers are crippled in their spiritual life by a fear of men and women. The key to deliverance from the fear of other people is a simple trust in God. He alone can give us that assurance that, even in the midst of wicked and violent men, we have nothing to fear since they cannot destroy our relationship with God. He will guard us until all eternity.

Prayer

Lord, through the ministry of the Holy Spirit in my life let my own attitude to you be righteous, filled with reverence and awe in your presence. Let your love drive away fear.

STUMBLING BLOCK

Isaiah 8: 14b-15
'For both houses of Israel he will be a stone that causes men to stumble and a rock that makes them fall. And for the people of Jerusalem he will be a trap and a snare. Many of them will stumble; they will fall and be broken, they will be snared and captured.'

Comment:

Isaiah was a realist. He was appalled at the political intrigues and in-fighting going on in Jerusalem. Despite all his exhortations to the people to trust in the Lord, the counsel of wicked men prevailed in the city. The fear of men outweighed their faith in God. The foreign policy followed by King Ahaz and his advisers was a disaster. Isaiah saw it as a denial of the sovereignty of God which could only lead to national disaster.

Isaiah knew that the purposes of God for his people are always good but that they could be frustrated by a lack of faith and by a spirit of rebellion. He saw evidence of spiritual wickedness throughout the nation. But worst of all, he saw it in the king and the rulers of the nation.

Ahaz went farther into spiritual apostasy than any other king of Judah, with the possible exception of Manasseh, his grandson. He even closed the Temple, nailing the doors shut so that it could not be used for worship, and 'set up altars at every street corner in Jerusalem' (2 Chronicles 28: 24).

It was in this context that the prophet saw God acting as a stumbling-block in Israel. He should have been the rock upon which they could stand with confidence and see his blessings flow through the nation. But the rock, upon which they could have stood in faith, had become for them an obstacle on their path of folly.

Paul quoted this verse in his letter to the Romans (9: 33). He interpreted it as a Messianic prophecy fulfilled in the coming of the Lord Jesus Christ. He saw Israel as guilty of rejecting the 'righteousness of God' which had been revealed through the advent of Messiah. Thus Jesus, who had been sent for the salvation of Israel, had become a stone of stumbling, 'a rock that makes them fall' (v 14).

The freedom of will which we have been given enables us either to choose the good or to reject it. If we reject the good, we are driven by evil. There is no middle path of compromise.

When the love of God and his way of righteousness are deliberately rejected this creates an environment of evil which gathers momentum in the nation. It affects the lives of all those who have neither consciously turned away from the ways of the world nor asked God to take control of their lives through the Lord Jesus.

Prayer

Father, open the eyes that are blind that your word may not be a stumbling-block to them but a rock of salvation. During this day, provide opportunities for me to share my faith in the Lord Jesus with others that they too may turn away from the ways of the world to the way of life.

WAIT FOR THE LORD

Isaiah 8: 16-17

Bind up the testimony and seal up the law among my disciples. I will wait for the Lord, who is hiding his face from the house of Jacob. I will put my trust in him.

Comment:

Chapters 7 and 8 form a distinct section in the prophecies of Isaiah. Its setting is the reign of King Ahaz and the war against Israel and Syria with the underlying threat of invasion from Assyria. The two verses in today's reading conclude this section.

The prophet presides over what resembles a legal ceremony in which he calls upon his disciples to witness the sealing up of the scroll on which were written the words that God had given him. This resembles an act in Jeremiah 32: 14 where the documents were sealed in a clay jar to preserve them for posterity.

Isaiah had gathered around him a group of disciples. They were probably like the 'company of prophets' whom we read about in 2 Kings 2: 7 who were led by Elisha. We know that both Isaiah and Jeremiah had a school of prophets who preserved their words and ensured that their teaching was passed on to the next generation.

Isaiah saw the inevitability of judgment coming upon a nation whose leaders and people had deliberately hardened their hearts to the word of God and turned away from the paths of righteousness, spurning the help that God freely offered in the face of grave danger from their enemies. As a consequence, God was hiding his face from the nation and leaving them exposed to their inevitable fate.

The sealing of the scroll was a sign of the inevitability of judgment, but it also meant that later on, when the catastrophe occurred, people would be able to see the true reason why it had happened and that God had clearly foretold its occurrence.

There are times in our lives when we stubbornly refuse to hear the truth or to accept that the path upon which we have embarked can only lead to catastrophe. The warnings given through godly friends, or through the stirring of the Spirit of God within us, are ignored in the pursuit of personal ambition or self-gratification. As a consequence, there comes a point where God simply hides his face from us until we are prepared to listen to him.

When this happens in the lives of those whom we love we can do no other than continue to pray for them fervently, showing them love and patiently waiting for the Lord to break through into their lives when they come to a realisation of the truth.

Prayer

Lord, I lift before you today those among my own loved ones who do not acknowledge you as Lord and Saviour. Bring them to a knowledge of the truth. Also, Lord, deal with any stubbornness in my own heart. With the Psalmist I pray, 'Reveal to me my hidden faults.'

LIVING WITNESSES

Isaiah 8: 18

Here am I, and the children the Lord has given me. We are signs and symbols in Israel from the Lord Almighty, who dwells on Mount Zion.

Comment:

Isaiah was the leader of a group of prophets, or disciples, who had gathered around him. He was also a family man and the names he gave to his children had prophetic significance. Each of these names conveyed a message to the nation. Shear-Jashub meant 'a remnant will return' or 'a remnant will survive', and Maher-Shalal-Hash-Baz meant 'quick to the plunder, swift to the spoil' (Isaiah 7: 3 and 8: 1).

Isaiah saw the whole of his life, and that of the prophetic community around him, as being an instrument in God's hands for conveying his word to the nation. He saw himself and all those with him as living witnesses for God. They were 'signs and symbols in Israel'.

Isaiah had done everything in his power to bring the word of God to the nation. Nevertheless, catastrophe lay ahead, though neither he nor his sons would experience it. The warning given to him at the time of his call to the prophetic ministry had already come true – the people had hardened their hearts and rejected the word of God.

The prophet, however, had also been shown that the hope of Israel lay in a remnant. Hence the significance in the names, given to his two sons. The nation would be plundered, but a remnant would return after a long time. The prophet and his family, which included his disciples, were signs to the nation.

God has chosen to use us as the means through which he communicates his word to the nation. Once we acknowledge Jesus as Lord of our life we are his living witnesses. We become 'signs and symbols' of the living God.

God can only use us as instruments in his hands if we are prepared to listen to him and to be obedient. Our lives have to reflect the holiness that is required of the servants of the Lord. There can be no compromise in the moral and spiritual standards required of those who represent the Father.

This is a particular word to those who have families. The family is a very special, God-given unit of primary spiritual significance. In the nation of Israel, it was of fundamental importance for prayer, worship and teaching. It was the responsibility of each family to teach their children all the things God had done for his people. This was part of the spiritual heritage of the nation that had to be preserved through the family.

Where there is healthy family life, children are brought up to know the Lord, to love him and trust him, and to be obedient to him. God is wanting each of us to be able to say, 'Here am I, and the children the Lord has given me. We are living witnesses to the presence of the Lord Almighty.'

Prayer
Father, help me today to fulfill the desire of your heart that I may be a faithful witness to the living God in the lives of those around me. Make my family a blessing to others, and my home a sanctuary honouring to you.

ENQUIRING OF GOD

Isaiah 8: 19

When men tell you to consult mediums and spiritists, who whisper and mutter, should not a people enquire of their God? Why consult the dead on behalf of the living?

Comment:

One of the major problems all the prophets had to confront, especially in the pre-exilic period, was that of idolatry. Some idea of the extent of occultic practices in the northern Kingdom of Israel may be gathered from reading 2 Kings 17. In that chapter the historian lists the reasons why God allowed Israel to be conquered by the Assyrians. All the things he lists, in fact, may be summarised under one word – 'idolatry'.

Isaiah was prophesying in the southern Kingdom of Judah at the same time as all these things were happening in the northern Kingdom of Israel. Judah was very little different from Israel in spiritual terms. Isaiah constantly had to battle against the occult forces and pagan practices that held the spiritual life of the nation in bondage. Necromancy, or consulting the dead, was a common practice.

It was not only the leaders of the nation who were not listening to the Lord on behalf of the nation, which was supposed to be in a covenant relationship with him, but the ordinary people consulted mediums and spiritists for guidance in their personal problems. In this verse the prophet explodes with indignation, 'Should not a people enquire of their God? Why consult the dead on behalf of the living?'

Today we live in an age of superstition when millions of

people consult their horoscope or obtain so-called 'life readings' from mediums, for themselves or their children. Even international leaders and members of royal families are reported to be in the habit of consulting clairvoyants before undertaking engagements. These practices are not only deeply offensive to God and indicate a lack of trust in him, they also open the door for demonic influences in our lives.

The temptation to consult mediums and spiritists in any form, even such mild forms as horoscopes, must be resisted if believers are to be faithful to God. There can be no compromise in this matter, for the enemy is prowling around and would love to gain a foothold in our lives or in the lives of members of our family or friends. This calls for constant vigilance.

Prayer

Lord, make me alert to any of the wily tactics of the enemy. Surround me throughout this day with the whole armour of God and the great shield of faith that I may not only be alert to danger but also have the power to resist temptation in any form.

SEEING THE LIGHT

Isaiah 9: 2-3

The people walking in darkness have seen a great light; on those living in the land of the shadow of death a light has dawned. You have enlarged the nation and increased their joy; they rejoice before you as people rejoice at the harvest.

Comment:

This is the beginning of one of the well-known messianic prophecies in Isaiah. He foresees the day coming when God would break into the course of human history and establish his presence in the world in a new and wonderful way. God would become incarnate in human flesh in order to accomplish the salvation of mankind which was part of his eternal purpose.

Isaiah sees the significance of this in the life of the nation Israel. He sees them as a people walking in darkness upon whom a great light suddenly floods. He sees the advent of the Messiah as transforming a people living under 'the shadow of death' into a people who have suddenly discovered life in all its fullness.

This contrasts vividly with the picture of gloom in the previous chapter where the prophet was foreseeing the terrible consequences of the disastrous foreign policy of Ahaz and his lack of faith in God. In today's reading Isaiah is looking beyond the national defeat, which he knows is inevitable, to the time of restoration when God would inaugurate a new era and wonderfully bless the remnant of Israel.

The prophet sees those upon whom the light has dawned as being filled with an almost inexpressible joy. He sees them rejoicing as people rejoice in an abundant harvest which assures them of plenty of food for the coming winter.

Once we have experienced the coming of Messiah into our life, everything changes. His presence radiates an incredible light that alters our perspective of everything. We move from darkness into light, from death to life, from ignorance to knowledge, from falsehood to truth. We now know the Messiah as Jesus our Lord. He brings a total transformation.

His presence radiates light and life and joy and peace. The difference is there for all to see. It cannot be hidden. Once Jesus comes into your life, his presence can be seen by all those around you.

This is true of new believers, but what about those who have known the Lord for many years? What about *your* life? Can the presence of Jesus be seen radiating through you?

Prayer
Lord, let the light of your presence and your love, joy and peace be seen in me today, to your glory and praise.

WONDERFUL COUNSELLOR

Isaiah 9: 6
For to us a child is born, to us a son is given, and the government will be on his shoulders. And he will be called Wonderful Counsellor, Mighty God, Everlasting Father, Prince of Peace.

Comment:

These are words which everyone who has ever attended a Christmas carol service must have heard! Isaiah was given the revelation that the advent of the Messiah would be as a tiny child. We have already read that one of his names would be Immanuel or 'God with us' (7: 14). In today's reading, we are told some of his other magnificent titles.

God himself would carry out his purposes of bringing salvation to all people by being born as a tiny, helpless, little baby. Upon his shoulders the government of the nations would rest. It is surely remarkable that God should entrust the government of the nations to a child. But what the prophet is emphasising is that this is the beginning of a new era in world history.

God's Messiah would be given many names including 'Wonderful Counsellor', which reminds us of the name Jesus used to denote the Holy Spirit (John 14: 16). The Messiah would give wise counsel to the nations to direct their steps into the way of righteousness that would lead to peace and prosperity.

The names which Isaiah declares for the Messiah reveal his divine nature. He is the 'Mighty God, Everlasting Father, Prince of Peace'. Each of these titles has particular significance for the Messianic reign on earth. The Messiah would be born with a human body, but he would also have the divine nature and exercise the power of the 'Mighty God'. He would care for the poor and the weak; to them he would be as an 'Everlasting Father', one who never leaves them and is always watching over them for good. His reign, upon his Second Coming, would also establish peace and justice in the world. Wars would cease and Messiah would be recognised as the 'Prince of Peace'.

If we are to have a healthy spiritual life, it is essential that we recognise the divinity of Christ. There can be no compromise or room for uncertainty over such a fundamental tenet in the Christian faith.

The claims Jesus made, such as, 'I and the Father are one' (John 10: 30) and, 'No-one comes to the Father except through me' (John 14: 6), are direct claims to equality with the Father. There can be no compromise.

We either accept Jesus as God or we dismiss him as a dangerous madman. The evidence of the Gospels is perfectly clear. He is the Messiah, our 'Wonderful Counsellor, Mighty God, Everlasting Father, Prince of Peace'!

Prayer

Fill me today, O Lord, with a sense of awe in your presence, for you are the Mighty One, the Living God, the Creator of all things, the giver and sustainer of life. Let me hear from you today, Wonderful Counsellor, that everything I do may be directed by you.

THE EVERLASTING KINGDOM

Isaiah 9: 7

**Of the increase of his government and peace there will be
no end. He will reign on David's throne and over his
kingdom, establishing and upholding it with justice and
righteousness from that time on for ever. The zeal of the
Lord Almighty will accomplish this.**

Comment:

Isaiah's conviction that the day would come when God
would send a great deliverer was unswerving. The
Messianic prophecies of Chapter 9 fall within the reign of
King Ahaz who was not simply a weak and wilful king –
he was deliberately wicked. He not only failed to trust the
Lord, the God of his fathers, but he actually introduced
pagan practices into the nation.

Ahaz sent a sketch of an altar which he saw in
Damascus and had it set up in the Temple and thus
deliberately introduced the worship of other gods (2 Kings
16: 10-14).

Ahaz was a disgrace to the very name of his great
ancestor, King David. Isaiah longed to see a king after the
stature of David who would uphold justice and
righteousness in the nation. In the figure of the great
Messianic deliverer he saw such a possibility. The contrast
between the Messianic king and King Ahaz could hardly be
greater.

It may be that Isaiah was seeing beyond the first coming
of Messiah, to his Second Coming when he would reign in
glory. In his first advent, Messiah came as a servant, thus
fulfilling the role foretold in Isaiah 53 where the servant
was 'despised and rejected', but nevertheless accomplished

his Messianic task of salvation through his personal suffering. In today's reading Isaiah foresaw the Messiah coming in glory to reign on David's throne and to extend his Kingdom with justice and righteousness to include all the nations.

No-one knows how near we are to seeing the Second Coming of our Lord and to the establishment of his government and everlasting peace upon earth. But one thing is sure – we may enter his Kingdom today.

The moment we make a conscious decision to allow Jesus to be king in our lives, we actually enter his Kingdom even though it is not yet established upon earth. We become part of the Messianic community, the body of Christ, the company of believers eagerly looking for his return. By submitting our wills and lives to his kingship, the Kingdom of God is further established.

We look forward to the day when 'the zeal of the Lord Almighty will accomplish this', when we become part of the first fruits of his Messianic reign and share in his joy.

Prayer

Father, we long for your Kingdom to come and your will to be done upon earth as it is in heaven. Enable me today to live as part of your Messianic community in whom you already rule with justice and righteousness. May all that I do this day be pleasing in your sight, to the honour of Christ Jesus, my Lord and King.

PRIDE AND ARROGANCE

Isaiah 9: 8a, 9-11, 12b

The Lord has sent a message against Jacob... All the people will know it... who say with pride and arrogance of heart. 'The bricks have fallen down, but we will rebuild with dressed stone; the fig-trees have been felled, but we will replace them with cedars.' But the Lord has strengthened Rezin's foes against them and has spurred their enemies on... Yet for all this, his anger is not turned away, his hand is still upraised.

Comment:

This is another prophecy from the time of King Ahaz, the evil king of Judah, although it is a message specifically for the northern Kingdom of Israel. Israel had entered into an alliance with Syria against Judah and the threat from their combined armies looked very menacing.

Foolishly, against the advice of Isaiah, Ahaz had sent to Assyria asking for help. The Assyrians needed no encouragement to attack Syria. They destroyed Damascus and assassinated King Rezin (2 Kings 16: 9). Clearly, Israel was next for invasion and Ahaz had precipitated this by sending to Nineveh for assistance.

The people of Israel were so spiritually blind and politically naive that they were still convinced that no disaster would fall upon them. With Syria on their northern flank gone they were exposed to the full might of the enemy. But they were still saying 'with pride and arrogance of heart' that, although part of the alliance had been broken down, there was nothing to worry about.

In fact they were actually boasting that they would not just rebuild their towns with ordinary bricks but with the finest stone! The one major factor in the situation which the people of Israel and their rulers failed to perceive was that God was actually allowing all these disasters to happen. They were signs of his anger against his people and he was using their enemies to convey a message to them, but they were deaf to it.

Once we get caught up in the world and find ourselves following the ways of the world, using the world's methods and committed to the world's values, we become blind to spiritual things. The values of the Kingdom are hidden from us or seen to be foolish.

Once the values of the world become dominant in our lives we find ourselves driven by them. This was the tragedy of Israel that led to her downfall. Pride and arrogance of heart soon create a barrier which separates us from God. Repentance is our only hope. It is the only way to re-establish the broken relationship with the Lord.

Pride and arrogance of heart are the most subtle of sins and are a constant temptation to those who have energy and initiative. The most vulnerable are the men and women with the greatest creativity and the most powerful gifting. The only protection is the whole armour of God and a close and humble walk with the Lord.

Prayer

Soften my heart, Lord. Keep me humble before you. Let my walk with you this day be close and guard me against pride and arrogance, through the Lord Jesus my Saviour.

HEAD AND TAIL

Isaiah 9: 13-16

But the people have not returned to him who struck them, nor have they sought the Lord Almighty. So the Lord will cut off from Israel both head and tail, both palm branch and reed in a single day; the elders and prominent men are the head, the prophets who teach lies are the tail. Those who guide this people mislead them, and those who are guided are led astray.

Comment:

This is the second of three prophetic poems in Chapter 9. They come from the period leading up to the invasion of Israel by the Assyrians and the destruction of Samaria in 721 BC. The three poems were addressed to the northern Kingdom of Israel, by Isaiah of Jerusalem, and they have been preserved by his school of prophets. Each of the poems ends with the editorial refrain, 'Yet for all this, his anger is not turned away, his hand is still upraised' (vv 12b, 17b, 21b).

Today's reading begins with the charge that the people were unresponsive to the signs sent to them by God: 'The people have not returned to him who struck them'. What was even worse in the eyes of the prophet was that they had not bothered to seek God. They had not taken the trouble to enquire if there were any word from the Lord. Even in the face of the imminent threat of invasion they had not turned to God. There were many other indications that the nation was not enjoying the blessings of God, yet they were quite unresponsive to any of these warning signs. 'Nor have they sought the Lord Almighty', was Isaiah's complaint.

The consequences of Israel's sin and spiritual blindness would be swift and devastating. The judgment of the Lord would fall upon both rulers and people; both head and tail would be cut off in a single day, or by a single blow. The whole nation would suffer together. The judgment would especially fall upon 'the elders and prominent men' whose policies had brought disaster upon the land.

The prophets, however, were equally guilty since they did not declare the word of God. In fact, they talked lies which were believed by both the rulers and the people. The elders were the head and the prophets were the tail. Both would be cut off on that day of judgment because they were guilty of misleading the people.

When a nation's rulers have no faith in God, the policies they devise are directed by human wisdom, which is often influenced by greed and selfish ambition. This was certainly true of Israel in the time of Isaiah. It was a time of great prosperity, so the rulers were self-satisfied and they ignored the signs of danger. But it was the religious leaders, the prophets, who should have been alert to danger. If they had faithfully declared the word of God, the nation might have repented and God would have protected them. Therefore, the religious leaders were the most culpable for the downfall of Israel.

This principle is still true today. God holds his own people – those who acknowledge him as their Lord – primarily responsible for the spiritual life of the nation. The task of the church, as the people of God, is to be the prophet to the nation. Are we really declaring the word of God in the land today? Or even to our own family and friends?!

Prayer

Father, raise up within your church those who will faithfully declare your word, and help me to be one of your faithful servants.

FIRE ALARM

Isaiah 9: 18-20a

Surely wickedness burns like a fire; it consumes briers and thorns, it sets the forest thickets ablaze, so that it rolls upward in a column of smoke. By the wrath of the Lord Almighty the land will be scorched and the people will be fuel for the fire; no-one will spare his brother. On the right they will devour, but still be hungry; on the left they will eat, but not be satisfied.

Comment:

This is the third of the prophetic poems which closes with the refrain, 'Yet for all this, his anger is not turned away, his hand is still upraised'. Isaiah of Jerusalem, although primarily a prophet to the southern Kingdom of Judah, was evidently familiar with the situation in Israel. He was probably a frequent visitor to Samaria and was deeply concerned with the wider international scene. He had opposed the possibility of Judah forming an alliance with Syria and Israel to fight the Assyrians.

Isaiah had advocated complete reliance upon God. King Ahaz of Judah had not entered the alliance, but he did something even worse. He sent envoys to Nineveh and made an alliance with the hated Assyrians. Isaiah foresaw that this would eventually bring disaster upon the land.

Each of these three poems is addressed to the northern kingdom and here he describes a time of judgment not only falling upon Samaria but upon the whole land of Israel. He sees it burning like a forest fire which consumes everything in its path: great trees, undergrowth, briers and thorn bushes, together with all the wildlife. He sees all living things being consumed. Once the fire takes a hold and gets out of control, it becomes unstoppable, especially if it is driven by a strong wind.

This picture of judgment coming upon Israel in the form of an all-consuming forest fire is a terrible picture of destruction. The prophet was foreseeing the indescribable suffering which would come upon the people. The smoke from a forest fire rises high into the sky and obscures the sunlight. It can be seen from hundreds of miles away. Its effect is to reduce the whole land to desolation. This was what Isaiah was seeing.

It is a warning message to us today. We often overlook the fact that 'fire' in the Bible is usually associated with judgment, not blessing. The coming judgment would reduce the countryside to a barren desert. The land would be unable to produce food for the people who would suffer the extremes of hunger. Isaiah saw this to be the result of the nation turning away from God and bringing upon themselves 'the wrath of the Lord Almighty'.

When a nation that is in a covenant relationship with God and knows the word of God, turns away from his teaching to practise all kinds of wickedness, that nation is in danger of severe judgment. When we apply this principle to our own nation we can see the danger facing us. Any nation that has had the word of God for centuries cannot claim innocence. We know the consequences for Israel of turning away from God, so we have no excuse. As Jesus said to the people of Jerusalem, 'unless *you* repent, you too will all perish' (Luke 13: 5).

Prayer

Lord, in your word you have said, 'In repentance and rest is your salvation, in quietness and trust is your strength' (Isaiah 30: 15). We pray for our nation today. Let your word be heard in the land. Cause the hearts of your people to turn to you, O Lord.

ROBBING THE POOR

Isaiah 10: 1-3

Woe to those who make unjust laws, to those who issue oppressive decrees, to deprive the poor of their rights and withhold justice from the oppressed of my people, making widows their prey and robbing the fatherless. What will you do on the day of reckoning, when disaster comes from afar? To whom will you run for help? Where will you leave your riches?

Comment:

This is the last of the seven woes addressed to the people of Judah. It has somehow became detached from the other six. Continuity requires that we read Isaiah 10: 1-4 following 5: 25. It completes the group by returning to the original theme of the wickedness of the rich and powerful who oppress the poor and powerless. It is a theme that occurs throughout the prophets and underlines God's hatred of injustice and oppression.

The prophet is clearly indignant at what he sees in the nation whereby those who hold political and economic power misuse it for their own selfish ends. They were making laws to favour the rich and 'to deprive the poor of their rights'. They oppressed widows and orphans, showing none of the compassion which the law, given to Israel through Moses, required. Deuteronomy 24: 14 clearly states, 'Do not take advantage of a hired man who is poor and needy, whether he is a brother Israelite or an alien living in one of your towns.'

Caring for the poor, even if they were foreigners, was not simply a matter of compassion, it was a matter of justice. Because God is just, he requires his people to be just. Justice, love and compassion are part of the very nature of God. They were part of the unique attributes that distinguished God from the idols worshipped by the pagans. The heart of Hebraic religion was to reveal the true nature of God. The Psalmist rejoiced in the tender compassion of God: 'My whole being will exclaim, "Who is like you, O Lord? You rescue the poor from those too strong for them, the poor and needy from those who rob them"' (Psalm 35: 10).

Jesus saw his own ministry in this same context of exercising tender care and compassion for the weak and the powerless. He identified with the prophecy of Isaiah 61: 1 – 'The Lord has anointed me to preach good news to the poor' – saying in the synagogue at Nazareth, 'Today this scripture is fulfilled in your hearing' (Luke 4: 21).

Jesus' compassion for the poor can be seen in the many accounts of his dealing with the blind, the beggars, the lepers, widows and children. Jesus showed great concern for the outcasts of society, such as the woman caught in the act of adultery, and for those who were despised and rejected by others. He knew that they were precious in God's sight. He himself was born in poverty and he identified with the poor and the powerless. Whatever you do, he said, 'for the least of these brothers of mine, you do for me' (Matthew 25: 40).

When, by our words or actions, we do not treat the humblest of God's children with love and compassion, we are not simply robbing the poor, we are robbing God.

Prayer

Lord, help me to show the same care and compassion for the weak as you showed. Soften my heart towards those for whom I should be caring.

NATIONS IN HIS HAND

Isaiah 10: 5-7, 12

'Woe to the Assyrian, the rod of my anger, in whose hand is the club of my wrath! I send him against a godless nation... But this is not what he intends... his purpose is to destroy, to put an end to many nations' ... When the Lord has finished all his work against Mount Zion and Jerusalem, he will say, 'I will punish the king of Assyria for the wilful pride of his heart and for the haughty look in his eyes'.

Comment:

This is an Eighth Century prophecy given in Jerusalem by the prophet Isaiah soon after the fall of Samaria and the destruction of the northern Kingdom of Israel by the Assyrians which took place in the year 721 BC. There was great anxiety in Judah and the fear that Jerusalem was next on Assyria's hit-list.

The prophet used this fear to bring a strong warning from God. 'As my hand seized the kingdoms of the idols, kingdoms whose images excelled those of Jerusalem and Samaria – shall I not deal with Jerusalem and her images as I dealt with Samaria and her idols?' (vv 10-11).

At the same time as he warned about the consequences of idolatry and unfaithfulness to God, Isaiah also declared his confidence in the universal sovereignty of God over all the nations. He saw God using a wicked pagan nation to bring judgment upon the sinfulness of his own people. But the day would come when he would turn and bring judgment upon that same wicked nation. Assyria was simply an instrument in his hands. At the moment God was using the Assyrians as a club in his hand to carry out his purpose of chastising Judah for her idolatry and unfaithfulness.

The Assyrians did not know that they were being used by God. They were proud and haughty, boasting in their strength and the might of their army. They believed it was due to their own prowess that they had conquered many of the small nations around them. They did not know that they could achieve nothing without the express permission of God who rules the nations and holds the whole universe in his hands. This is the lesson that Isaiah was seeking to teach Judah.

God sometimes allows the wicked to oppress his own people when they have been unfaithful or forgetful of him. It is not his desire that we should suffer but, throughout the Bible, suffering is used redemptively to bring God's people closer to the Lord.

The New Testament reminds us that God himself suffered for us and that he is with us in suffering. The time will come when he will deal with the evil oppressors, for he holds the nations in his hands 'as a drop in a bucket' (Isaiah 40: 15). In the meantime we should allow adverse circumstances to draw us closer to God, who never abandons us whatever the circumstances.

Prayer

Father, I know that you are the Almighty One who holds the nations in your hands; you are the God of history and you are all-powerful. Lord, I thank you that you have taught us to call you Abba, Father, to know your tenderness and your care for each one of your children. Help me to carry with me throughout this day the knowledge of your all-powerful presence.

PAGAN PRIDE

Isaiah 10: 15-16

Does the axe raise itself above him who swings it, or the saw boast against him who uses it? As if a rod were to wield him who lifts it up, or a club brandish him who is not wood! Therefore, the Lord, the Lord Almighty, will send a wasting disease upon his sturdy warriors; under his pomp a fire will be kindled like a blazing flame.

Comment:

This prophecy is linked with yesterday's reading which declared that, when God had finished using the pagan king of Assyria to carry out his purposes, he would punish him. Today's reading gives the reason why God will do this. The answer is encapsulated in one word – pride.

The pride of man is abhorrent to God. The pagans, who fear neither God nor man, boast in their own strength, in the power they exercise and their ability to control the lives of others.

This prophecy is a reminder that, ultimately, all power comes from God and when the boastful pagan tyrant over-reaches himself his downfall is assured. Isaiah prophesied the downfall of Assyria: 'The Lord Almighty will send a wasting disease upon his sturdy warriors'. This did, in fact, happen just a few years later when the Assyrians laid siege to Jerusalem.

There is a stirring account of the humiliation suffered by the Assyrians and the downfall of Sennacherib in 2 Kings 19: 20-37. King Hezekiah of Judah received a boastful and threatening message from Sennacherib calling for the surrender of Jerusalem. He warned Hezekiah against trusting in his God since none of the gods of the other nations had been able to save them from the destructive power of the Assyrian army.

Hezekiah, a man of great faith, took the letter into the Temple and 'spread it out before the Lord'. He sent a message to the prophet Isaiah and received a wonderfully uplifting prophecy in response, in which God promised that the Assyrians would not enter the city of Jerusalem because the Lord would defend it. Sennacherib had gone too far in his boastful pride. He had insulted God. As a result, most of his army died of a plague (Isaiah 37: 36).

As believers, it is so easy for us to get caught up in the ways of the world. We work among pagans; the media bombards us with pagan values and we too can begin to forget God and to take pride in our own achievements, our influence, our worldly status or our material possessions.

We take pride in our comfortable home or our lovely family, our good looks, our attractive personality. There are a thousand ways in which the subtle sin of pride can create a cancer in our spiritual lives. Our prayer today is in the words of Psalm 51: 10-12.

Prayer

'Create in me a pure heart, O God, and renew a steadfast spirit within me. Do not cast me from your presence or take your Holy Spirit from me. Restore to me the joy of your salvation and grant me a willing spirit, to sustain me.'

TRUST IN GOD

Isaiah 10: 20-21
In that day the remnant of Israel, the survivors of the house of Jacob, will no longer rely on him who struck them down but will truly rely on the Lord, the Holy One of Israel. A remnant will return, a remnant of Jacob will return to the Mighty God.

Comment:

Isaiah was prophesying in the wake of the destruction of the northern Kingdom of Israel. This defeat must have been a shattering blow to the people in the tiny southern state of Judah and to the people in the city of Jerusalem where Isaiah was ministering. When he got into the presence of the Lord to seek understanding of the terrible events in the northern half of the divided kingdom, he could see that it was the sinfulness and faithlessness of the people which had brought about their downfall. 'Destruction has been decreed, overwhelming and righteous' (v 22). Isaiah could see the justice of what had happened to Israel, brought about by their own lack of trust in God.

Despite the tragedy, the prophet knew that God was still in control and that the day would come when he would restore Israel to the land. But it would be only a small remnant who would return. This was inevitable because Sargon, after overthrowing Samaria in 721 BC, deported thousands of its citizens and settled them across the Assyrian Empire.

In their new environment most of the captive Israelites would soon have lost their identity and married into the local community. Their distinct heritage as descendants of Jacob and their faith in the God of Israel would have been lost.

There are times when we simply have to bear the consequences of our own actions. It is even harder when we have to bear the consequences of the actions of others and we feel ourselves to be the innocent victims. There were many innocent people in Israel who had not bowed their knees to idols but who nevertheless suffered when the ruthless Assyrian armies over-ran the land.

As individuals they were innocent but they suffered when the sinfulness of their leaders brought judgment upon the whole nation. This is the hardest kind of suffering to bear.

The Lord solemnly promises that those who are faithful will be kept through times of tragedy, hardship or persecution – even in martyrdom he preserves the souls of those who belong to him. This is the message of the prophets and it is affirmed throughout the New Testament in the teaching of Jesus and the witness of the apostles.

In the letters to the seven churches of Revelation (Chapters 2 and 3) there is a reference in each of them to 'him who overcomes'. The letters were written for those suffering hardship and persecution.

Through these letters the Lord Jesus gave a solemn promise that the 'overcomers' would not lose their salvation under any circumstances. God would keep them close to himself and guarantee them eternal life in his loving presence, provided they did not deny their faith in the Lord.

Prayer

Lord, help me to be one of your overcomers; to be numbered among the faithful remnant of your people. Keep me close to you this day and may my faith be unfaltering, my loyalty unswerving and my witness to your love and faithfulness pleasing in your sight, through Jesus Christ my Lord.

GOD'S PROMISE

Isaiah 10: 24-25

Therefore, this is what the Lord, the Lord Almighty, says: 'O my people who live in Zion, do not be afraid of the Assyrians, who beat you with a rod and lift up a club against you, as Egypt did. Very soon my anger against you will end and my wrath will be directed to their destruction.'

Comment:

This prophecy follows yesterday's reading and is in the context of the destruction which had come upon the northern Kingdom of Israel. Samaria had been destroyed and the people had been deported and scattered across Mesopotamia.

The people in the tiny southern Kingdom of Judah were terrified that the Assyrians would now sweep down upon them and Isaiah was assuring them that they had nothing to fear, so long as they put their trust in the Lord. God had promised that he would defend them. The Assyrians would 'shake their fist at the mount of the Daughter of Zion, at the hill of Jerusalem' (v 32), but they would not succeed in their attack because the Lord Almighty would break their power.

The Assyrian armies would not be able to break through Jerusalem's defences because the wrath of God would be directed towards their destruction. The people of Jerusalem had no need to be afraid of the Assyrians who were only men. So long as their trust was in God and they were faithful to him, they had nothing to fear.

This is a prophecy within a prophecy. The whole passage is addressed to 'the remnant of the house of Israel, the survivors of the house of Jacob' (v 20). It is set in an apocalyptic/Messianic context as seen in the opening phrase, 'In that day'. It envisages a time coming when God will judge the nations in righteousness. He will overthrow the nations that have oppressed Israel, and will enable a remnant to return from exile.

The people of Jerusalem are included in the promise to Israel because, in the Messianic age, the kingdom will again be united – 'The people of Judah and the people of Israel will be reunited, and they will appoint one leader' (Hosea 1:11a). The prophet foresaw God rising to deal with the enemies of his people. He guaranteed their future with the promise, 'In that day their burdens will be lifted from your shoulders, their yoke from your neck' (v 27).

The day of God's judgment of the nations will bring the downfall of all those who trust in the politics of power and violence. When he establishes the reign of the Prince of Peace, 'of the increase of his government and peace there will be no end' (Isaiah 9: 7).

God's promises to us are from everlasting to everlasting. He is faithful to carry out his promises even when all the circumstances surrounding our lives are threatening and everything appears to be going wrong. So long as we keep our trust in him we have nothing to fear. He will keep us safe by his side. His love and faithfulness are our guarantee. Always remember that however much the nations rage and the enemy at our gate appears to triumph, the Lord wins in the end. His Kingdom will come!

Prayer

Father, how can we ever thank you adequately for all your goodness and your faithfulness in fulfilling your promises? May your love surround me today and may all that I do be pleasing in your sight that I may praise you not only with my lips but with my life.

PROMISE OF MESSIAH

Isaiah 11: 1-3a

A shoot will come up from the stump of Jesse; from his roots a Branch will bear fruit. The Spirit of the Lord will rest on him – the Spirit of wisdom and of understanding, the Spirit of counsel and of power, the Spirit of knowledge and of the fear of the Lord – and he will delight in the fear of the Lord.

Comment:

This prophecy is looking beyond the destruction of Jerusalem and the exile in Babylon to a time of restoration. The prophet takes it as read that the monarchy is effectively finished, despite the fact that the royal line of David, whose descendants had ruled the nation for many generations, was to be preserved as Matthew shows in the genealogy of Jesus (1: 12-16).

Isaiah had foreseen this coming for a long time. He had warned and pleaded with the nation to put their trust only in the Lord and to remain faithful to him, but in the end he knew that the sinfulness of men would drive the nation to destruction.

In this prophecy he foresees a time coming when a new king would emerge to lead the nation. He sees it like a huge tree cut down by the woodman's axe leaving only a stump showing above ground, yet from this stump there emerges a new green shoot with the promise of new life, fresh growth and fruit.

The new king would come from the line of David and the Spirit of the Lord would be upon him. The Spirit would give him wisdom and understanding so that he would be able to lead the nation wisely, which clearly most previous kings had not done. The Spirit would also give him the counsel, or guidance, of God and the power of God to rule wisely and to fulfil the will of the Lord. The Spirit would also give him knowledge and the fear of the Lord.

In Hebrew thought 'knowing' and 'knowledge' are not mere intellectual processes, but they include being involved in, or the realisation of, actions appropriate to that knowledge. Thus, to know God is not merely to have a sense of awe, but to live in an appropriate way. This is beautifully expressed in Proverbs 3: 5b-6a and 7b, which urges the reader to 'lean not on your own understanding; in all your ways acknowledge him... fear the Lord and shun evil'.

Knowing God enables the believer to understand the purposes of God and the way he is fulfilling them. This is what Jesus meant when he said that he was calling his disciples 'friends' rather than 'servants'. Jesus said that a servant doesn't know his master's business. By contrast he was making everything he had learned from the Father known to his followers (John 15: 15).

We demonstrate our love of God by our obedience to him and our care for others. As John says, 'If anyone says, "I love God", yet hates his brother, he is a liar' (1 John 4: 20). In the same way our knowledge of God should include understanding his purposes for us and for our generation. We should therefore be living as 'children of light' and not of darkness. We should be those who know God and who not only fear to disobey him but long to please him.

Prayer
Lord, we long to see your will done on earth as it is in heaven. Give me today not only a sense of awe in your presence, but also the power to do your will. I know that it is only your Holy Spirit who can do this and make the difference in my life – please fill me afresh right now.

RIGHTEOUSNESS AND FAITHFULNESS

Isaiah 11: 3b-5

He will not judge by what he sees with his eyes, or decide by what he hears with his ears; but with righteousness he will judge the needy, with justice he will give decisions for the poor of the earth. He will strike the earth with the rod of his mouth; with the breath of his lips he will slay the wicked. Righteousness will be his belt and faithfulness the sash round his waist.

Comment:

This prophecy is a continuation of the passage which formed yesterday's reading. Isaiah is looking ahead to the time when Messiah will come and he sees the effect of the Spirit of the Lord upon him which will prevent him from being deceived in the way that most people are. 'He will not judge by what he sees with his eyes.'

This reminds us of the account in 1 Samuel 16 of the prophet going to inspect the family of Jesse. Samuel believed that among Jesse's sons he would find the Lord's chosen one whom he would anoint as king.

When he saw the eldest, a fine strong lad, he thought, 'Surely the Lord's anointed stands here before the Lord. But the Lord said to Samuel, "Do not consider his appearance or his height, for I have rejected him. The Lord does not look at the things man looks at. Man looks at the outward appearance, but the Lord looks at the heart"' (vv 6b-7).

God's Messiah is foreseen in this prophecy as exercising discernment so that he is able to judge with righteousness. His concern will be to defend the poor and the powerless from the exploitation of the wicked who delight to oppress them.

This is an expansion of the promise in 9: 7 that the Messiah will be a descendant of King David who will establish a reign of righteousness and justice. In fact even Messiah's clothing will reflect the righteousness and faithfulness that are essential parts of his nature. 'Righteousness will be his belt and faithfulness the sash round his waist.'

We are surrounded by deception in all our dealings with the world. The voice of the deceiver is often soft and enticing. The ways of evil appear attractive.

It is only as we buckle on the belt of righteousness, and draw the cloak of faithfulness around us through the indwelling power of the Holy Spirit, that we are able to resist the wiles of the enemy.

Our faithfulness to God and our righteousness do not depend upon our cleverness but upon the work of the Spirit of God within our lives.

Prayer

Lord, guard me throughout this day from those who seek to deceive me. Keep me strong in the face of temptation. Do not let the enemy triumph over me or let my feet slip from the path of righteousness. Let your Spirit be upon me and clothe me with righteousness and faithfulness, through Jesus Christ my Lord.

NATURE TRANSFORMED

Isaiah 11: 6-9
**The wolf will live with the lamb, the leopard will lie
down with the goat, the calf and the lion and the yearling
together; and a little child will lead them. The cow will
feed with the bear, their young will lie down together,
and the lion will eat straw like the ox. The infant will
play near the hole of the cobra, and the young child put
his hand into the viper's nest. They will neither harm nor
destroy on all my holy mountain, for the earth will be
full of the knowledge of the Lord as the waters cover the
sea.**

Comment:

This beautiful picture of peace and harmony can hardly
fail to move even the hardest hearts. The whole world
is longing for peace; even the men of violence declare that
the achievement of peace is their real objective! Dictators
say that they are eliminating those who oppose their rule in
order to establish peace in the land.

This prophecy looks ahead to the establishment of the
Messianic Kingdom when God will bring all things under
his rule. It foresees the time coming when the generations
of mankind will have run their course and reached a climax
of evil and destruction.

At that point God will intervene to establish his reign.
God, who originally created the whole world as a place of
beauty, peace and love, will interpose his will on the course
of human history, to re-establish his divine authority over
the whole created order.

In this prophecy Isaiah is foreseeing the time coming
when God will send his Messiah to establish his authority

upon earth. He will not only subdue the warring nations but also harmonise the whole natural order of creation so that there will be peace between the wolf and the lamb, the calf and the lion. Even the infant will be safe from the snake.

This beautiful picture of the Messianic Kingdom is part of the expectation of Christians for the Second Coming, or Parousia, of Christ. When he comes in power and glory he will inaugurate the Kingdom in which his followers will share with him in his Messianic glory.

We do not know when the Lord will come again and Jesus himself warned us against trying to forecast the date of his Parousia. He told us instead always to be ready, watching and living in prayerful expectation of his coming.

The true believer longs for the day when 'the earth will be full of the knowledge of the Lord'.

Prayer

Lord, help me to live this day in expectation of your soon coming to establish your rule of righteousness upon the earth. Until then, keep me faithful and watchful, longing for your Kingdom of righteousness. Give me the opportunity today to witness to others concerning the hope that is within me, through Jesus Christ my Lord.

SECOND REGATHERING

Isaiah 11: 10-12

In that day the Root of Jesse will stand as a banner for the peoples; the nations will rally to him, and his place of rest will be glorious. In that day the Lord will reach out his hand a second time to reclaim the remnant that is left of his people from Assyria, from Lower Egypt, from Upper Egypt, from Cush, from Elam, from Babylonia, from Hamath and from the islands of the sea. He will raise a banner for the nations and gather the exiles of Israel; he will assemble the scattered people of Judah from the four quarters of the earth.

Comment:

Any prophecy that begins, 'In that day' is clearly referring to divine intervention usually eschatological in nature – that is, referring to the end of the age or the last days. This is a Messianic prophecy, no longer referring to a shoot or branch coming out of the stump of Jesse, but to the root itself. So the prophecy refers to God establishing his rule on earth after the pattern of an idealised reign of King David.

The prophet foresees the Jewish people being regathered to the land from all the nations around the Mediterranean and all the far away places where they have been scattered. Clearly this could not refer to the return of the exiles from Babylon in 520 BC, but to a second regathering from places where they had not been scattered in the time of Isaiah or for three or four hundred years after that.

It was not until the destruction of Jerusalem by the Romans in 70 AD and their rape of Judea that the greatest dispersion of the Jewish people began. It was completed after the Bar Kokhba revolt of 135 AD, and it is only since the establishment of the modern State of Israel in 1948 that large numbers of Jews have been returning to their ancient homeland from all over the world.

This prophecy foresees that at the time of this second regathering, Israel will appear as a banner for the nations. A banner is something that can be seen from far away. The eyes of the nations would be upon the land as God regathered the scattered exiles.

Since the second regathering of Jews to the land began soon after World War II and the re-establishment of the State of Israel, the eyes of the world have been constantly focused upon that tiny piece of land. But this prophecy says that it will be the Messiah himself who will be the focus of the attention of the Gentile nations. When the day of the Lord comes the whole world will see him and acknowledge his sovereign rule – that has yet to be fulfilled. But the regathering of Israel had to happen first.

Paul looks forward to the day when, 'at the name of Jesus every knee should bow... and every tongue confess that Jesus Christ is Lord' (Philippians 2: 10-11a).

As believers, we look forward to the coming Kingdom when Christ will return. But we also recognise that the Kingdom has already begun – we enter it the moment we trust in Jesus. Even death cannot separate us from him.

Whatever our circumstances he will keep us until that day when he presents us before his Father.

Prayer
Lord, we look forward to the day when all the world will acknowledge your Lordship. As I have put my trust in you, O Lord, keep me close to you and reassure me that nothing can separate me from your love, through Messiah Jesus.

STRENGTH AND SALVATION

Isaiah 12: 1-3
In that day you will say: 'I will praise you, O Lord. Although you were angry with me, your anger has turned away and you have comforted me. Surely God is my salvation; I will trust and not be afraid. The Lord, the Lord, is my strength and my song; he has become my salvation.' With joy you will draw water from the wells of salvation.

Comment:

This prophecy is part of a song of praise in which the prophet foresees the people singing as they are regathered to the land of Israel. It is in a similar sense to the 'Song of Ascents' in the Psalter (Psalms 120-134). The people returning from exile are seen pouring out their thanksgiving to God who had saved them.

The praise is expressed in the first-person-singular as was customary in Israel. Although the whole community of the remnant of the nation who were returning were giving thanks to God, their praise was not impersonal. It is significant that they did not sing '*we* praise you, O Lord'.

The whole company of the redeemed was in unity, but *each one* offered praise and thanksgiving to God as an individual expression of their heartfelt thanks. Hence they sang '*I* will praise you, O Lord'.

The phrase 'in that day' indicates that this is an apocalyptic vision that is foreseeing God intervening in the course of human history to clear the enemies of Israel out of the land which he had promised to their fathers for ever. It comes at the climax of the prophecies in Chapters 9 to 11 which foretell the time when God will destroy the world-power of evil and establish his reign of peace and justice on the earth.

Just as Moses, Miriam and all the people sang a song of thanksgiving for their release from slavery in Egypt (Exodus 15), so the 'redeemed of the Lord' will, 'in that day', sing a hymn of praise as they see God working out his purposes among the nations and fulfilling his promises to his people. They will praise God for saving them from the suffering they have endured in exile and for comforting them.

Nothing gives the believer greater joy than to see God at work in the world, bringing comfort, healing and salvation to people. When we see him at work in our own life and in the lives of those around us, we cannot help singing, 'The Lord is my strength and my song, he has become my salvation.'

The reference to drawing from the wells of salvation reminds us of Jesus' promise to give living water to those who trust in him: 'The water I give him will become in him a spring of water welling up to eternal life' (John 4: 14).

Prayer

Lord, we want to be among those who constantly praise you. Today I will trust and not be afraid because you are my strength and my salvation. Enable me throughout this day to draw water from your well of salvation that I may be filled with joy and inner strength.

SING FOR JOY

Isaiah 12: 4-6

In that day you will say: 'Give thanks to the Lord, call on his name; make known among the nations what he has done, and proclaim that his name is exalted. Sing to the Lord, for he has done glorious things; let this be known to all the world. Shout aloud and sing for joy, people of Zion, for great is the Holy One of Israel among you.'

Comment:

This is the second half of the great eschatological song of praise which we began yesterday. It is the song which the prophet foresaw that the people would sing as they returned to the land of Israel from exile.

In this Messianic hymn of praise the people of Israel give thanks to God because he has fulfilled his promises to overcome the wicked nations who had been oppressing his covenant people. So the world can no longer ignore 'the Holy One of Israel'.

What he has done will be known to the whole world and it will gain great glory for his name. His name will be exalted among the nations. The God of the Universe, who chose the little insignificant people of Israel for his own special purposes, will at last use them to reveal his glory throughout the world.

Later, in the time of the Second Temple, the song was was probably also used by people making a pilgrimage to Jerusalem singing the songs of Zion as they travelled.

It is in a similar sense to the 'Song of Ascents' in the Psalter (Psalms 120-134). As they sang and gave thanks to Almighty God the pilgrims would have found that their praises took away the weariness of walking along mountain paths or dusty tracks and it took away the fear of being attacked by robbers. It turned the attention of the pilgrims away from the things of the flesh and the world, and focused their eyes upon the Lord.

We all go through difficult times when the road seems long and hard and our present circumstances seem unending. We grow weary and discontented with our lot. It is at these times when it is even more important to praise the Lord. As we do so we find there are many things for which to thank him that we had overlooked.

As the pilgrims exalted the name of the Lord they remembered all the glorious things he had done, so they began to shout aloud and sing for joy. Isaiah foresaw the whole company of the returning exiles exalting the name of God as they recalled his great deeds. The more energetic among them even danced. No doubt even the most weary felt like doing so!

This can be our experience even in the midst of difficult times. We are still able to bear a good witness to others around us because of the inner joy we have. There is nothing quite like the 'joy of the Lord'. Like his peace, it 'passes understanding'!

Prayer

Lord, I want to thank you today for all the good things you have done in my life. I want to let all the world know how good you are and to exalt your name. Put a new song in my heart today and fill me with joy so that everyone I meet may experience your blessing through the presence of Jesus my Lord.

GOD'S PURPOSES

Isaiah 14: 25-27

'I will crush the Assyrian in my land; on my mountains I will trample him down. His yoke will be taken from my people, and his burden removed from their shoulders.' This is the plan determined for the whole world; this is the hand stretched out over all nations. For the Lord Almighty has purposed, and who can thwart him? His hand is stretched out, and who can turn it back?

Comment:

This is the conclusion of a short prophecy about Assyria. The prophecy declares that God will crush the Assyrians in the land of Israel. It is one of many instances where the land of Israel is referred to as 'my land' and the mountains of Israel as 'my mountains'. It underlines the fact that the people of Israel did not own the land. The land belonged to the Lord and the people were his stewards, and were therefore responsible to him for their husbandry. But they did not occupy the land unconditionally. The conditions were (and still are) obedience and trust in God.

It was God's intention to humble the pride, and to break the power, of the mighty Assyrian army in the tiny land of Israel. This would be a demonstration of the universal sovereignty of God; his power over all the nations and over the whole of creation. He had allowed the Assyrians to triumph over the northern Kingdom of Israel because this was part of his purpose in allowing judgment to fall upon the wickedness of his rebellious people. But in due time God himself would intervene to punish the cruel, unjust and oppressive regime of the Assyrians.

This was all part of God's plan for the nations. He had

plans for the whole world which could not be thwarted. Once God had announced his purposes nothing could stand against him or stop him from fulfilling his word. His hand was stretched out over the nations and even the apparently invincible army of the Assyrians could not prevent God from carrying out his plan.

This understanding of God as the Lord of history is something which many people in the rich industrialised nations of the West have largely lost today. There is not much direct evidence of the activity of God in busy city streets, or in the world of commerce and industry. It is easy to overlook the fact that God is still working out his purposes among the nations.

Just as the mighty Assyrian army fell in the days of Isaiah so the mighty Communist empire of the Soviet Union began to fall in 1986 when God stretched out his hand and said that the time to end that evil empire had come – 70 years after the Bolshevik revolution of 1916.

Moreover, the Lord continues to work out his purposes, in our time and before our eyes, for the tiny nation of Israel. Whilst many Israelis are still in unbelief, God is at work, faithful to his promises. He will accomplish his plans for the honour of his mighty name.

God not only has a plan for Israel and all the nations, he also has a good plan for the lives of each of his children. Our greatest desire should be to seek that plan and to allow God to fulfil his purposes in our lives, for therein lies our greatest happiness and fulfilment.

Prayer
Father, help me to understand your plans for Israel and the whole world and the way you are working out your purposes among the nations and in my own life.

THE KINGDOM OF GOD

Isaiah 16: 4b-5

The oppressor will come to an end, and destruction will cease; the aggressor will vanish from the land. In love a throne will be established; in faithfulness a man will sit on it – one from the house of David – one who in judging seeks justice and speeds the cause of righteousness.

Comment:

This short prophecy comes in the middle of a much longer pronouncement concerning Moab. It foresees a time when the whole land of Moab will be overrun by an enemy who will bring about great destruction and loss of life.

The longer prophecy occupies the whole of Chapters 15 and 16. It foresees the destruction of the famous vineyards of the Heshbon area (16: 8-10) when the anticipated joy of the harvest is stilled and an eerie silence descends upon the whole area.

The prophecy also foresees many refugees making their way across the Jordan into Israel and seeking refuge there. Lambs are sent as a sacrificial offering to God in Jerusalem and ambassadors are also dispatched to plead for the safety of the refugees (16: 1-4).

The major purpose of this apocalyptic vision which is given to the prophet is, once again, to demonstrate that God is in control of the nations, that he is the Lord of history. The climax comes in the verses we have taken for our reading today. It foresees a time when God will intervene in the affairs of humanity and restrain the oppressor.

'Destruction will cease; the aggressor will vanish from

the land.' God will establish his reign, which will be a time of peace and security for all people, because his throne will be established in love as well as in righteousness (v 5).

The one who will administer justice to all the nations will come from the house of David. He will establish righteousness which will benefit the whole of mankind. This is similar to the vision of Isaiah 2 where the word of the Lord goes out from Jerusalem: All people go to him seeking justice and he establishes peace among the nations.

This is surely the ultimate vision of all the nations. But while there are many who cry 'peace, peace', it is only God who is able to establish true peace. He alone can change the hearts of men and women and banish the greed, selfishness and violence that are the causes of oppression.

Christians know that God has already established his reign upon earth and we can enter the Kingdom of God the moment we accept Jesus as Lord of our lives. Peace with God is the only basis for true peace with humanity.

Prayer
Father, may your Kingdom come and your will be done on earth as it is in heaven. May your peace reign over my life throughout this day, through Jesus my Lord.

THE END OF IDOLATRY

Isaiah 17: 7-8, 13

**In that day men will look to their Maker and turn their
eyes to the Holy One of Israel. They will not look to the
altars, the work of their hands, and they will have no
regard for the Asherah poles and the incense altars their
fingers have made. Although the peoples roar like the
roar of surging waters, when he rebukes them they flee
far away, driven before the wind like chaff on the hills.**

Comment:

These two verses read almost like an aside in the flow of
apocalyptic prophecy which runs right through this
section of Isaiah from Chapter 13 to 23. Their subject is the
sovereignty of God who is in control of the nations and
guiding the course of human history.

The prophet focuses upon one nation after another of
the neighbours of Israel. They are Babylon, Assyria,
Philistia, Moab, Syria, Ethiopia, Egypt, Edom, Arabia and
Tyre. Each of them will one day be judged by the Lord who
is the God of Creation and the one who established the
nations in their lands.

The prophet sees a day coming when the violent and
rebellious nature of humanity will reach such a point that
the very existence of the whole world will be threatened.
This is expressed in 17: 12 as 'the raging of many nations –
they rage like the raging sea!' The next verse expresses the
apocalyptic vision of God establishing his rule on earth.

In our reading today the prophet turns aside from the
great vision of God bringing the nations before him for
judgment, to make the almost unnecessary observation
that, in that day, all idolatry will disappear. The world-

shattering events will be so intense and all-embracing that the eyes of all people in all the nations will turn to their Maker who is, of course, the 'Holy One of Israel'.

In that day the great deception will end, the scales will fall from the eyes of all humanity so that they will no longer regard material things as having any ultimate worth. They will despise the things that their own hands have made.

When we come to know God as our Father, and the Lord Jesus as our Saviour, life is transformed and all our values change. It is like a short-sighted man putting on spectacles – suddenly all the blurred images around him become clear!

Whereas at the moment, this is true for believers who have experienced new birth through Christ, in the day foreseen by the prophet, this will be the experience of all humanity.

The Apostle Paul foresaw the same scene when, before God, 'every knee will bow' – echoing Isaiah 45: 23 – and everyone will acknowledge the rule of God in the world and his authority over each life.

Prayer

Reveal, O Lord, any areas of my life which are not surrendered to you. Where there is idolatry, or an over-emphasis upon the value of material things, make it plain to me so that I may turn away from things that have no real value. Father, throughout this day make me so aware of your presence that I may turn away from anything that is not pleasing in your sight.

FORGOTTEN GOD

Isaiah 17: 10-11

You have forgotten God your Saviour; you have not remembered the Rock, your fortress. Therefore, though you set out the finest plants and plant imported vines, though on the day you set them out, you make them grow, and on the morning when you plant them, you bring them to bud, yet the harvest will be as nothing in the day of disease and incurable pain.

Comment:

Today's reading is probably linked with yesterday's which was also on the theme of idolatry and represents a diversion from the prophet's main theme which is an apocalyptic vision of the time when God will judge all the nations. The difficulty with these two verses is that, although they come in the middle of the chapters dealing with the Gentile nations surrounding Israel, they are clearly addressed to people who are in a covenant relationship with God. The prophet would never say, 'You have forgotten God your Saviour' to the people of Damascus, because they had never known him.

Most scholars believe that, at this point in his survey of the Gentile nations, Isaiah broke off and declared a message to the people of Jerusalem. He was reminding them that they themselves would not escape the judgment of God in that day when he calls all the nations to account. Even those who are believers, who are the Lord's own people in a covenant relationship with him, are accountable to God. The Apostle Paul emphasises this in Romans 2: 5-11. In fact, he says that when God judges all human beings it will be a case of 'first for the Jew and then for the

Gentile'. All will come before the bar of judgment in the day of the Lord.

It would appear that this same principle was revealed to the prophet Isaiah and, when telling the people of Judah the events he foresees occurring in the last days, he looks with horror upon the evident idolatry in the land among his own people who have forgotten God and not remembered the one who is their rock and their fortress. The use of these words is reminiscent of many similar passages in the Psalms such as, 'He alone is my rock and my salvation; he is my fortress, I shall never be shaken' (62: 2). It is, in fact, from this same Psalm that Paul quotes in Romans 2: 6 in laying down the principle that 'God does not show favouritism' (2: 11).

Isaiah reminds the people of Jerusalem that if they turn away from God, however much energy and effort they expend, they will never succeed in producing a good harvest. And on the day when all the nations are engulfed in trouble, violence, disease and pain, they too will not be spared.

It is a salutary message concerning our accountability before God. Once we know him as our Father and have received him as our Saviour, if we are faithless and turn away from him, we too will not be able to stand firm in the day when trouble breaks out throughout the unbelieving nations. None of us knows when that day will come. It is his desire that we should always be ready, alert, watching and praying for the Lord's return.

Prayer

Father, keep me alert to the way you are working out your purposes in the world. May it never be said of me that I have forgotten you, for you are indeed my rock and my fortress; and in you alone there is salvation, through Jesus your precious Son.

THE BANNER OF THE LORD

Isaiah 18: 3

All you people of the world, you who live on the earth, when a banner is raised on the mountains, you will see it, and when a trumpet sounds, you will hear it.

Comment:

A traditional interpretation of Isaiah 18 by biblical scholars links it with a contemporary situation in the time of King Hezekiah when envoys came to Jerusalem from Egypt and Ethiopia. They came to discuss with King Hezekiah the proposal to form a political and military alliance against the Assyrians. Even if that was the time when this prophecy was given, it should still be seen in the context of the apocalyptic revelation given to Isaiah concerning the things that would be coming upon the nations in the last days when God brings them all before him for judgment.

Our reading today speaks of a time when God will raise a banner on the mountains which will be seen by all people. Today, we are part of a generation who, for the first time in the history of the world, are able to see this prophecy literally fulfilled. Through the medium of television it is possible for people in every part of the world to see a banner raised on the mountains of Israel. In 1999 it was reported that a camera had been mounted on the Mount of Olives in Jerusalem focused on the Golden Gate and transmitting onto the Internet so that people all over the world could be 'watchmen on the walls of Jerusalem', waiting to see the return of Messiah.

This prophecy in Isaiah, however, also has a symbolic meaning. The banner was widely used in Isaiah's day for military purposes. When the army went into battle the king raised his banner to show his troops where he was so that they could rally to his presence.

The apocalyptic significance of this is that, in the last days, God will raise up the tiny land of Israel in such a way that the eyes of all the world will be focused upon it. Events in the land of Israel will indicate the presence of God working out his purposes in the world. All the nations will see it and will hear of it.

This verse is of great significance since it represents the earliest revelation in the Bible of what, in the New Testament, is known as the 'signs' of the end-times which are detailed by Jesus in Matthew 24, Mark 13 and Luke 21. They are also referred to by other New Testament writers such as Peter, who says that when we perceive the signs indicating the nearness of these events we should ask the question, 'What kind of people ought you to be?' Peter himself answers this, 'You ought to live holy and godly lives as you look forward to the day of God and speed its coming' (2 Peter 3: 11-12).

It is this question that forms our thought for today. Since the tiny land of Israel is rarely out of world news and many of the events referred to in scripture are beginning to take place in our lifetime, we should be asking the question, 'what sort of people should we be?'

Prayer

Father, we know that we should be living holy and godly lives. Cleanse and purify your servants that we may more perfectly reflect your holiness and that you may be able to use us to fulfil your purposes and to show forth your glory.

A SIGN IN EGYPT

Isaiah 19: 19-21a

In that day there will be an altar to the Lord in the heart of Egypt, and a monument to the Lord at its border. It will be a sign and witness to the Lord Almighty in the land of Egypt. When they cry out to the Lord because of their oppressors, he will send them a saviour and defender, and he will rescue them. So the Lord will make himself known to the Egyptians, and in that day they will acknowledge the Lord.

Comment:

Most of the apocalyptic chapters of Isaiah 13 to 23 are written in poetry, but our reading today comes from a short passage written in prose, Isaiah 19: 16-25. In some translations of the Bible it is printed in a different typeface so that it is distinguishable from the main thrust of the poetic prophecy. The prose passages are written as a kind of explanation of the prophecy.

Our reading today explains the spiritual significance of what will happen in Egypt on the day when God brings all the nations before him for judgment. The poetic prophecy is in Isaiah 19: 1-15 and the explanation is in verses 16-25.

The prophecy says that there will be revolution in Egypt (v 2) which will result in confusion, idolatry, necromancy (v 3) and a despotic ruler will arise (v 4). There will be a great drought (vv 5-6) and famine (vv 7-10) and the Egyptians will be helpless (vv 11-15). The reference to 'a sign and witness to the Lord Almighty in the land of Egypt' is usually thought to indicate the presence of Jews of the Diaspora in Egypt. When the nation is shaken this gives them the opportunity to witness to the Lord, the Holy one of Israel who is God of all the world.

The outcome of God shaking the nations will be that the Egyptians will acknowledge the Lord and actually establish an altar to him in their land. God himself will respond to their cries and will rescue them from the cruelty of the oppressor. This will establish his honour and glory among the Egyptians as he becomes known to them and they acknowledge his Lordship over all the earth.

This is God's ultimate purpose for every human being, that all should come to know him and acknowledge him as Lord and Saviour. Isaiah received another similar revelation when he heard God say, 'Before me every knee will bow; by me every tongue will swear. They will say of me, "In the Lord alone are righteousness and strength"' (45: 23b-24a).

Paul received further revelation that the Father would fulfil his purposes to bring all people to himself through Jesus. Paul foresaw the day coming when 'at the name of Jesus every knee should bow, and every tongue confess that Jesus Christ is Lord' (Philippians 2: 10-11). Even those who had not willingly acknowledged his name before the Parousia will be forced to recognise his Lordship. His name will be honoured throughout all the nations.

Prayer

Father, help me today to acknowledge you as Lord and Saviour. Overrule in all my conversations and activities today through the indwelling power of your Holy Spirit. May all that I do and say be pleasing in your sight this day. I ask this through Jesus Christ my Lord.

PEACE AT LAST!

Isaiah 19: 23-25
**In that day there will be a highway from Egypt to
Assyria. The Assyrians will go to Egypt and the
Egyptians to Assyria. The Egyptians and Assyrians will
worship together. In that day Israel will be the third,
along with Egypt and Assyria, a blessing on the earth.
The Lord Almighty will bless them, saying, 'Blessed be
Egypt my people, Assyria my handiwork, and Israel my
inheritance.'**

Comment:

Our reading today is one of the most significant
revelations in the whole of the Hebrew scriptures. It
occurs in the context of prophecies concerning what will
happen to Egypt in the day of the Lord, when God brings
all the nations of the world before him for judgment.
Leading up to that day will be a time of tremendous
instability and upheaval among the nations, such as the
wars and revolutions and other apocalyptic events
described by Jesus in Luke 21: 9-11.

In this passage, which concludes Chapter 19, the
prophet is shown that the purpose of the shaking of the
nations is not primarily for punishment, but ultimately for
salvation! The violent political and social upheavals in
Egypt, referred to in 19: 2, will cause great suffering among
the Egyptians in which the Jews of the Diaspora will share.
As they cry out to the Lord for help, he will answer them
by sending a saviour to rescue them (v 20).

This will be a powerful witness to the Egyptians who
will acknowledge the God of Israel to be the one true and
only God of all the world. Thus the sufferings endured by

the Jews actually lead to the salvation of pagan nations.

The prophet sees that this is the principle of salvation which God is working out on a world-wide basis. This is the reason why he has allowed his covenant people to be scattered among all the nations. Their suffering thus has a redemptive purpose. It will be used by God as the means of bringing salvation to people in all the nations. This is a theme that is developed later in Isaiah where Israel is described as the 'servant of the Lord' (42: 19) and becomes personified in the Messiah in Chapter 53.

Isaiah foresees the Egyptians and Assyrians, sworn enemies, being brought together as one people through their acceptance of the one Lord and Saviour whom they worship together. Thus Israel becomes a blessing to all the peoples on earth.

This was the promise that God gave to Abraham after he had proved his absolute trust in the Lord by his willingness to sacrifice his only son Isaac. The promise was, 'Through your offspring all nations on earth will be blessed, because you have obeyed me' (Genesis 22: 18).

As the gospel of the Kingdom of God is being preached throughout the world, the day will come when Jesus will come again and establish peace, and reconcile the nations. We are privileged to have a share in this harvest as we tell others the good news of God's purposes.

Prayer
Father, make me a blessing to others throughout this day. Enable me to tell others of your wonderful plan for all people. Help me to radiate the joy of your presence throughout this day.

ON THE THRESHING FLOOR

Isaiah 21: 8-10

The lookout shouted, 'Day after day, my lord, I stand on the watchtower; every night I stay at my post. Look, here comes a man in a chariot with a team of horses. And he gives back the answer: "Babylon has fallen, has fallen! All the images of its gods lie shattered on the ground!"' O my people, crushed on the threshing-floor, I tell you what I have heard from the Lord Almighty, from the God of Israel.

Comment:

In today's reading we hear the prophet describing what he sees as the climax of his apocalyptic message, events in the last days when God brings all the nations of the world before him. What he sees is so staggering that his whole body is racked with pain (v 3). It was like being dealt a physical blow that knocked him to the ground. He says, 'My heart falters, fear makes me tremble; the twilight I longed for has become a horror to me' (v 4).

What God had revealed to the prophet concerning the events in the last days was so terrible and horrific that he simply could not cope with the message. In order to understand this message it is important to remember that, for the Israelites, the twilight was the sign of dawn. The lengthening shadows meant that the sun was about to go down on the old day and the new day was about to begin. In Israel, the new day begins when the sun sets, not when it rises. The prophet had longed for the day of deliverance, but what he saw caused him to recoil in horror.

In a vision he saw the news being brought to Jerusalem that Babylon had fallen. The city which symbolised the world of violence, wickedness and oppression had at last been overcome, but at what cost! Isaiah was no doubt seeing the same vision as the Apostle John describes in Revelation 18: 2. John records the revelation of Jesus that an angel with a loud voice shouted, 'Fallen! Fallen is Babylon the Great! She has become a home for demons and a haunt for every evil spirit'.

Isaiah saw that God's own covenant people also go through the days of great tribulation. A literal translation of v 10 is, 'O my threshed one, child of the threshing-floor, I tell you what I have heard.'

The prophet saw the suffering of the Jews on the threshing-floor of world history. He saw that it was the purpose of God to allow them to be bruised and wounded as was the Suffering Servant of Isaiah 53 and as was the Lord Jesus in the Crucifixion.

The message of the cross foreshadowed here is that believers sometimes find themselves going through a 'threshing-floor' experience, that is, a time of suffering. But the suffering of those who remain faithful to the Lord under all circumstances is mightily used by God in his redemptive purposes for the whole of humanity.

We, none of us, welcome suffering, but God is always alongside us strengthening and upholding us. He will never leave us alone and he will never forsake us.

Prayer

Lord, make me one of your overcomers. Give me the strength to remain faithful under all circumstances. Increase my faith and enable me to stand firmly, surrounded by your whole armour, through Jesus Christ.

DAWN WATCH

Isaiah 21: 11-12

Someone calls to me from Seir, 'Watchman, what is left of the night? Watchman, what is left of the night?' The watchman replies, 'Morning is coming, but also the night. If you would ask, then ask; and come back yet again.'

Comment:

Today's reading presents commentators with many difficulties. These are due to the uncertain meaning of the introduction, 'Someone calls to me from Seir'. Seir is the range of mountains to the south-east of the Dead Sea which means that the prophecy is associated with Edom. Biblical scholars wonder why anyone would be calling out from Edom to a watchman in Judah! The distance is too great to make this a practical possibility. The most usual explanation is that this has a symbolic or spiritual interpretation.

There is, however, another solution. Edom was one of the neighbouring states surrounding Israel which was also occupied by the Babylonians and which was suffering similar oppression. The prophet was answering the questions which he knew were being asked in Edom as well as in Israel: 'When will Babylon fall? When will the time of oppression and suffering be over?' The whole region was suffering under the heel of Babylon, which had become a byword for cruelty and injustice.

The questioner is clearly impatient for an answer since the question is repeated before the watchman has the opportunity of responding. 'What is left of the night?' he asks. In other words, 'What time is it? How much longer must we endure the terrors of the night, and the cruel injustices that have descended like a dark cloud covering the whole region?' This question is also echoed in the cry of the souls of the martyrs in Revelation 6: 10, 'How long, Sovereign Lord, holy and true, until you judge the inhabitants of the earth and avenge our blood?'

The question is really about God's timing. When is the day of the Lord's deliverance coming? When will he intervene to correct the injustices done to the powerless? When will he provide for the poor and the weak? The prophet's response is that the morning is certainly coming although it is still night-time. There were still some difficult times to go through, but the prophet was reassuring the people that, even though the darkness still surrounded them, God would undoubtedly fulfil his promises. The daylight would soon appear.

The watchman also said, 'Don't be afraid to keep asking.' The implication is that God does not resent us asking questions. There is a similar message in Isaiah 62: 7 where the intercessors are exhorted to give God no rest until he establishes Jerusalem. As a loving Father, God wants us to talk to him about the problems of life and the things that are beyond our human understanding.

When we find ourselves in an oppressive situation from which there seems to be no relief, it is right to call out to the Lord and to keep on asking for his help. The assurance is here that he has heard and he will heed the prayer of faith; morning is coming, it is coming very soon! There is not much of the night left so do not lose heart and, above all, never cease to pray!

Prayer

Hasten the day, O Lord. Let the night pass and the new day dawn when the prayer of faith will be answered. Hasten that day, O Lord, in the name of Jesus our Lord and Saviour.

LOOKING TO THE CREATOR

Isaiah 22: 10-11
**You counted the buildings in Jerusalem and tore down
houses to strengthen the wall. You built a reservoir
between the two walls for the water of the Old Pool, but
you did not look to the One who made it, or have regard
for the One who planned it long ago.**

Comment:

Today's reading is particularly interesting because it refers
to an actual historical event, and yet it is in the setting of
the eschatological prophecies focusing upon all the nations
surrounding Israel. This international survey which runs
through Chapters 13-23 includes a prophecy concerning
Jerusalem (Chapter 22). This is all part of the prophet's
intention in declaring to the people of Judah the things that
God has revealed to him. His objective is to show what will
happen in the last days when God will bring all the nations
before him for judgment. This includes events in and around
Jerusalem which will be the centre point in the divine activity.

It is God's intention to reveal his very nature and
purposes to all the unbelieving nations surrounding the
land of Israel by the miraculous things that he does in that
land. The prophet foresees the time coming when all the
nations will gather to attack Jerusalem because that city
symbolises the presence of God and the nations themselves
are in rebellion against him.

In repelling the onslaught and defeating his enemies
God demonstrates his universal power as Creator of the
Universe who holds the nations in his hands as a 'drop in a
bucket' (Isaiah 40: 15). Isaiah was thus looking forward to
the day when all the nations will recognise God and

138

declare that he is the one and only God of all the world.

In our reading today Isaiah recalls how the people of Judah made desperate attempts to shore up the defences of Jerusalem before the siege of the Assyrian army in 701 BC, but the one thing they did not do was to look to God to whom the city belongs. This was the reason why every city in Judah had suffered terrible destruction. All their preparations had been useless. Even Jerusalem had been humiliated, although the city was saved from destruction by divine intervention (2 Kings 19: 35).

Judah had joined the general revolt against Assyria in 705 BC. She and the neighbouring nations were relying upon Egypt for help, but this did not come and Hezekiah had to strip the Temple of its treasures as well as hand over the leading men and women of the city in order to buy peace from Sennacherib. The people had done everything humanly possible to defend the city, except the one thing they should have done – look to the Lord for help and put their trust in him.

This incident is a reminder of the truth stated in Psalm 127, that unless the Lord builds the house its labourers work in vain. All our activities, careful planning and expenditure of wealth and energy are really useless unless we seek the Lord first of all to know his plans for the city, or the nation, or our individual lives. The principle is the same, God's plans for us are good, but if we ignore him and try to live our lives without him we bring disaster upon ourselves.

Prayer

Father, forgive us for the times we have ignored you; the many times we have not looked to you or had regard for your plans. Enable me today to keep my eyes upon you, to keep my ears open to the prompting of your Holy Spirit, that in all I do I may be in the very centre of your will. I ask this through Jesus Christ.

TIME TO WEEP AND TIME FOR JOY

Isaiah 22: 12-13
The Lord, the Lord Almighty, called you on that day to weep and to wail, to tear out your hair and put on sackcloth. But see, there is joy and revelry, slaughtering of cattle and killing of sheep, eating of meat and drinking of wine! 'Let us eat and drink', you say, 'for tomorrow we die!'

Comment:

Today's reading is a severe rebuke brought by the prophet Isaiah that is linked with yesterday's reading. The historical circumstances are the humiliating defeat inflicted by the Assyrian emperor Sennacherib upon Judah in the time of King Hezekiah. The city of Jerusalem surrendered without a fight. In fact, all the army and officials had attempted to escape during the siege and had simply been captured and executed or shot in the back with an arrow while fleeing (see 22: 1-3).

Despite all the preparations they had made for the siege the city was unprepared because they had not looked to the Lord and he alone as their true defender. Isaiah saw this as a little prototype and warning for the great battle that would come in the last days when God brings all the nations before him for judgment. The prophet sees that Jerusalem will be at the centre of the great world upheaval when nation rises against nation, and he is using the defeat at the hands of Sennacherib as a vivid warning of the necessity to listen to God and only to do what he says.

The Lord had called for repentance and humility before him. It should have been a time of weeping and crying out to the Lord. Instead there was joy and revelry, eating and drinking. People were saying, 'Well, we might as well get drunk tonight because it is inevitable that the city will fall and we will die'. There was a kind of fatalism that had gripped some of the people. Others had gone up onto the roofs of their houses and were shouting with joy because the Assyrian army had withdrawn, probably because they had heard a rumour that an Egyptian army was coming against them.

Isaiah, however, was noting the cost, the thousands who had been killed in battles around Jerusalem, and in Lachish and other cities, as well as the devastation of the land. This should not have been a day of drunken revelry but of mourning. The prophet also knew that the Assyrians would be back, as indeed they were a short time later.

The prophet was saying that if they had listened to the Lord and cried out to him he would have been their defender, but he would not defend an unrighteous city. The holiness of God demands that he will not defend an unholy people.

We can only be confident in the blessings of the Lord and his protection over our lives if we are walking with him in humility, being careful to keep to the paths of righteousness. If we do not take time to listen to him and to be obedient to his word we cannot expect to see his loving protection and blessing over our lives or in the life of the community or nation.

Prayer

Lord, I want to give this day into your hands so that throughout its hours I may be conscious of your presence. Help me to hear what you are saying and to be guided by your Holy Spirit in all the decisions and conversations I may have, through Jesus Christ my Lord.

A STRONG WARNING

Isaiah 24: 1-3

See, the Lord is going to lay waste the earth and devastate it; he will ruin its face and scatter its inhabitants – it will be the same for priests as for people, for master as for servant, for mistress as for maid, for seller as for buyer, for borrower as for lender, for debtor as for creditor. The earth will be completely laid waste and totally plundered. The Lord has spoken this word.

Comment:

The whole of Isaiah 24 is known as the 'Little Apocalypse', meaning that it describes an end-time scenario in figurative language. Nineteenth and early twentieth century biblical scholars usually dismissed this chapter as a flight of prophetic fantasy far removed from reality. They could not imagine a destructive power great enough to fulfil this prophecy.

Since the mid-twentieth century, with the advent of atomic weapons of mass destruction, it is quite conceivable that the earth could, quite literally, be laid waste. Scientists have warned that an international nuclear war could result in a 'nuclear desert' which would render large areas of the earth uninhabitable.

The prophets of Israel believed in God's absolute sovereign control of the whole universe; nothing happened without his divine approval. Therefore, they said that if the wickedness of mankind reached the ultimate depths of devastating the whole earth, it would be because God had allowed it to happen; it would be part of his will for mankind at that time. Thus, in describing the scene of devastation which he saw in a prophetic vision as he interceded before the throne of God, the prophet said that God would do this.

The prophets of Israel made no distinction between what God allowed and what he actually did by direct action. For them it was one and the same thing. It was simply different ways in which God chose to accomplish his purposes. For the prophet, there was no difference between saying, 'The Lord is going to devastate the earth' and saying, 'Wicked men will lay waste the earth.'

The task of the prophet was to warn that unless men and women are redeemed, they will eventually destroy themselves and the world around them. The forces of evil are so great and powerful that mankind is powerless to resist them alone and unaided. The prophet foresaw the forces of destruction gaining such a hold over mankind that unless God intervenes to save them the whole earth will be destroyed. This is one of the great unfulfilled prophecies of scripture and it is a solemn warning to the world.

Once we allow sin to take control of our lives we are driven by the destructive forces of evil. God awaits our repentance before stepping in to break 'the power of cancelled sin' as Wesley describes it.

God has already done this in the lives of countless millions of believers and he is longing to do it for the whole of mankind. It was for this purpose that he sent his only begotten Son, our Lord Jesus, the Messiah.

Prayer
Lord, how easy it is for us to fall into sin. We acknowledge that we often fail to see the consequences of the little sins which we commit or of our wrong attitudes as we drift away from you. Help us, Father, by holding on to us, cleansing us and restoring a right attitude within us.

POLLUTING THE EARTH

Isaiah 24: 5-6
**The earth is defiled by its people; they have disobeyed
the laws, violated the statutes and broken the everlasting
covenant. Therefore a curse consumes the earth; its
people must bear their guilt. Therefore earth's inhabitants
are burned up, and very few are left.**

Comment:

This passage illustrates the interpretation we gave with
yesterday's reading. We said that the Hebrew prophets
made no distinction between what God allowed and his
direct actions. In yesterday's reading the devastation of the
earth was all referred to as the work of God. Today's
passage is the opposite. The defiling, or polluting, of the
earth is all said to be the activity of human beings.

The reason given for devastation coming upon the earth
is that the people 'have disobeyed the laws' of God, as a
result of which 'a curse consumes the earth' and 'its people
must bear their guilt'. The RSV translates this passage, 'The
earth lies polluted under its inhabitants'. This emphasises
the physical as well as the spiritual defilement of the land,
the air and the sea.

The current world situation whereby the environment is
being polluted by the activities of mankind is consistent
with the situation foreseen by the prophet. The earth, the
atmosphere, seas and rivers are all suffering massive
pollution. But the world is also being defiled by the
wickedness of men and women, through violence, the vast
shedding of innocent blood, as well as the moral pollution
that is spread through the media and through the Internet.

We live in a generation that has no concern for the law

of God or his statutes and commands. Yet there is no excuse even though people do not know God through our Lord and Saviour. As Paul says, 'What may be known about God is plain' (Romans 1: 18-20), so, as Isaiah foresees, 'people must bear their guilt'.

It sounds a very harsh judgment. Yet the prophet is simply warning in the most forceful language about what he foresees as the inevitable consequences of sin. The 'curse' he refers to is the sin which is inherent in our human nature.

We can only be released from this by entering into a new relationship with God through the Lord Jesus, our Messiah. It was his death on the cross that has released the power which enables each one of us to be freed from the destructive power of sin. But we have to be willing to receive the power of the Holy Spirit.

As soon as we recognise our plight and cry out to God for help, he responds. When we trust in the name of Jesus he brings into our lives the loving release that we need. This enables us to experience a new dimension of life. It brings to us the peace of God, which sustains and guards us, even when all the earth around us is being polluted by evil.

Prayer
Grant me this day, loving Father, your peace which passes all human understanding. Let your presence go with me so that the turmoil of the world is not able to rob me of the joy of your presence.

HE SHALL REIGN

Isaiah 24: 18b-23

The foundations of the earth shake. The earth is broken up, the earth is split asunder, the earth is thoroughly shaken... So heavy upon it is the guilt of its rebellion... In that day the Lord will punish the powers in the heavens above and the kings on the earth below... The moon will be abashed, the sun ashamed; for the Lord Almighty will reign.

Comment:

This is one of the most dramatic prophecies in scripture where the prophet describes, in vivid language, a vision of terrible destruction coming upon the earth. It engulfs the whole world and is the direct result of the rebellion of the nations who are heavy with guilt.

The whole purpose of this prophecy is to highlight the victory of God over the wickedness of mankind. Despite the highly descriptive reference to the shaking of the nations and the very foundations of the earth, followed by the scene of judgment which God will bring upon the evil powers in the heavenlies and upon the rulers on earth, the climax of the prophecy is the reign of the Lord Almighty. The glory of God will outshine the moon and the sun when he overcomes the powers of evil and establishes his supreme authority on earth.

The prophet sees the inevitability of a time of judgment coming upon the nations. God will have to judge them one day, but his intention is to inaugurate the Messianic reign. The day will come when God will raise the standard of the Lord on Mount Zion in Jerusalem. This is fully in line with the teaching of Jesus that a time of judgment will precede his own coming again in glory. His reign on earth will eclipse the brightness of the sun and the moon.

Many believers today seem to have lost confidence in the Second Coming of Christ. But that expectation has been held among Christians since the days of the Early Church. Moreover, there are more prophecies in the Bible concerning the Second Coming of Messiah than those relating to his first coming!

Many people in recent years have been disillusioned by the false predictions of dates, especially in the years leading up to the end of the second millennium. But God always fulfils his promises and the signs that Jesus said we should watch for are becoming increasingly obvious (see Matthew 24: 1-14 and Luke 21: 5-28).

A time of great turmoil is coming upon the world before the Second Coming of our Lord. All people will be shaken. So, too, will all organisations and institutions, including the church.

But believers should rejoice because they know that when the shaking becomes evident throughout the world this will be the sign that the Lord's coming is near. The day of his mighty victory over the nations and glorious reign is at hand.

Prayer

Loving Father, hold your children close to you during the gathering storm among the nations. Take away all fear and enable your people to live in simple trust knowing that you will ultimately triumph over evil.

THE FALL OF BABYLON

Isaiah 25: 1-3

O Lord, you are my God; I will exalt you and praise your name, for in perfect faithfulness you have done marvellous things, things planned long ago. You have made the city a heap of rubble, the fortified town a ruin, the foreigners' stronghold a city no more; it will never be rebuilt. Therefore strong peoples will honour you; cities of ruthless nations will revere you.

Comment:

The great shaking of the nations described in Chapter 24 is followed in this passage by a song of thanksgiving and praise to God. It seems a little strange that this is in the first-person-singular, whereas later references (25: 9 and 26: 1) make it clear that all the people join in singing the song.

The most likely explanation is that the prophet himself was recoiling at the fearful scene of turmoil and destruction he was foreseeing in Chapter 24. When that reaches its climax with the revelation of its purpose – 'for the Lord Almighty will reign on Mount Zion and in Jerusalem' (24: 23) – the prophet then breaks into spontaneous praise: 'I will exalt and praise your name'.

You can almost feel the prophet's sense of relief that, after all the terrible things he has been shown, he is now privileged to see the climax of history as God establishes righteousness, peace and justice in the world.

These things were 'planned long ago'. This is the way God intends to fulfil his purposes. The great event that brings to an end the tyranny of wickedness, that has held the whole of mankind in chains throughout the ages, is the destruction of the world capital. This is the significance of the statement, 'You have made the city a heap of rubble'.

It is quite wrong to interpret this, as some commentators have done, as the city of Jerusalem. The city in this prophecy is 'the foreigners' stronghold' and certainly not the city of God. No prophet would rejoice in the destruction of Jerusalem even though, like Jeremiah, he foretold such an event.

This passage is part of the end-times scenario in which God intervenes in human history to overcome the power of evil and to establish his reign. When his action is seen, and his almighty power is recognised, all the Gentile nations will turn to the Lord and acknowledge him. Nations hostile to the reign of God and who have persecuted his people for centuries will at last honour God.

It may be that the prophet identified the city to be destroyed as Babylon which had become a symbol of evil and oppression, but it is not named. In fact what is envisioned is the symbolic Babylon, what Jesus called 'Mammon', the power of wickedness in the world.

This passage encapsulates the hope of all true believers. The day of the Lord will come; the day when the Father will send the Son to judge the nations and establish his Kingdom. As the evil in the world increases there are many signs that the day is not far off. The day of rejoicing of God's people draws near.

Prayer
Lord, you are 'a refuge for the poor' and 'a shelter from the storm' for all who love and trust you. Keep me close to you throughout this day.

WIPE AWAY TEARS

Isaiah 25: 6-8

On this mountain the Lord Almighty will prepare a feast of rich food for all peoples, a banquet of aged wine – the best of meats and the finest of wines. On this mountain he will destroy the shroud that enfolds all peoples, the sheet that covers all nations; he will swallow up death for ever. The Sovereign Lord will wipe away the tears from all faces; he will remove the disgrace of his people from all the earth. The Lord has spoken.

Comment:

This is a beautiful prophecy of a great banquet which God prepares for his people drawn from all the nations. It is another scene in the end-time scenario that the prophet has been describing in the 'Isaiah apocalypse'. It links with the teaching of Jesus, and especially his parables of the Kingdom, such as 'the great banquet' of Luke 14: 15f, where the poor, the crippled, the blind and the lame are brought in to share in the feast.

The prophet foresees God hosting this wonderful mountain-top feast which will be the climax of world history as he establishes his reign on earth. At that time God will remove 'the shroud' that covers the nations and keeps people at enmity with each other and fills the world with bloodshed, strife and suffering. As God breaks the power of sin which envelopes the whole world, he removes the cause of suffering and begins to wipe away the tears from the faces of his people.

The 'shroud' also symbolises mourning. It represents the head-covering of women mourning the loss of husbands and sons killed in war or having died a natural death. It is linked with the promise that God will 'swallow up death forever'. He will deal with sin that is the root of all the madness that drives the nations to war with each other, to slaughter the flower of the nation's youth, to enslave, dominate and oppress one another, through family feuds, ethnic cleansing and international war.

How futile and pointless is all this hatred and strife! When will we learn to respect one another, to be gentle with the weak, to share with the poor, and to care for others? The answer given in the Bible is that this will not happen until God deals with sin; until he sends the Lord Jesus to judge the nations and to establish his reign of peace. Then he will wipe away all tears.

As a father loves his own precious children, so the Lord has compassion upon those who are suffering, the victims of violence, those who are hated, rejected and feel unloved. God tenderly wipes away their tears and enfolds them securely in his arms.

We do not have to wait for the 'end-times' to experience this wonderful love of God. We can have it now! That is the good news that Jesus came to bring.

Prayer
Dearest Lord, thank you that when we go through times of trouble and sadness you never leave us. Wipe away the tears and keep me from self-pity in testing times. Enable me to live in the power of your victory over sin and death. May that be my experience throughout today.

REJOICE AND BE GLAD!

Isaiah 25:9
In that day they will say, 'Surely this is our God; we trusted in him, and he saved us. This is the Lord, we trusted in him; let us rejoice and be glad in his salvation.'

Comment:

In this verse the prophet is foreseeing God's great victory over the forces of evil. Through his conquest of sin and death, God removes the blanket of rebellion that for centuries has covered the people of the world. As the Lord wipes the tear-stained faces of his people, they look up into his face and say, 'This is the Lord! We trusted in him; let us rejoice and be glad!'

The final promise in the prophecy we looked at yesterday was that 'he will remove the disgrace of his people from all the earth' (v 8). The prophet was foreseeing the day when God will establish his Kingdom on earth and deal with the central problem of the sin of mankind. In so doing he vindicates his own people who are faithful to his word and who love and serve him despite persecution.

The world scorns and derides men and women of faith. They are rejected by evil men, but the Lord will remove their disgrace and establish them in righteousness. This is why there will be such rejoicing among believers as they see the Lord fulfilling his promises. Their suffering has not been in vain and they fill the earth with shouts of joy.

So we hear the shout, 'This is our God! We trusted him, let us rejoice and be glad!' It is the spontaneous outburst of praise from those who suddenly find themselves liberated from some terrible situation which has imprisoned them. They are like men and women set free from slavery. They know this has not come about through anything that they have done or any merit, or righteousness of their own.

It is this experience of unmerited salvation that causes such rejoicing. This same experience overwhelms the new believer who accepts Jesus into his or her life. It comes as an almost incredible realisation that through the cross Jesus has actually lifted the whole burden of guilt. God has not only forgiven, but actually blotted out the past.

This is what the prophet is foreseeing. He himself is entering into the wonderful experience of liberation which sinful men and women feel as God breaks the power that imprisons them. No wonder they rejoice!

Every day should be a day of thanksgiving and rejoicing for the believer who lives in the love of the Lord and trusts in him. Unbelievers find it amazing that Christians can actually rejoice in times of hardship and suffering. They simply do not understand the 'joy of the Lord' that wells up within the believer like a never-ending stream.

This was the experience of the prophet Jeremiah when he was grieving over the terrible events he had witnessed with the fall of Jerusalem to the cruel Babylonian army. He wrote, 'Because of the Lord's great love we are not consumed, for his compassions never fail. They are new every morning; great is your faithfulness' (Lamentations 3: 22-23).

The true believer can always find something for which to give thanks!

Prayer
Lord, help me to live throughout today rejoicing in your liberating, loving, forgiving presence. I praise your name and bless you, Father.

PERFECT PEACE

Isaiah 26:1-4

**In that day this song will be sung in the land of Judah:
We have a strong city; God makes salvation its walls and
ramparts. Open the gates that the righteous nation may
enter, the nation that keeps faith. You will keep in perfect
peace him whose mind is steadfast, because he trusts in
you. Trust in the Lord for ever, for the Lord, the Lord, is
the Rock eternal.**

Comment:

The theme of 'rejoicing in the Lord' is carried forward
into Chapter 26. This is all part of the 'end-times'
scenario foreseen by the prophet. The context is God
bringing judgment upon the earth. He breaks the power of
evil over the lives of men and women and establishes his
Kingdom of righteousness. The response of those who have
stood firm and remained faithful through the times of great
turmoil and shaking of the nations is to break out into
spontaneous songs of praise. They cannot restrain their
thanksgiving to the living God for the salvation of his
people.

The prophet is continuing the theme begun in 25:1,
where the song of praise centred around the 'marvellous
things' God had done in making 'the city a heap of rubble'.
The city envisaged is the world power of evil and the
prophet foresees God fulfilling the 'things planned long
ago' by overcoming evil. In so doing God liberates his
faithful people from the bondage in which they are held by
the wickedness of the world.

The phrase, 'Open the gates that the righteous nation
may enter', echoes the song of the pilgrims in Psalm 24: 9,

'Lift up your heads, O you gates... that the King of Glory may come in.' Similar words are found in Psalm 118: 19: 'Open for me the gates of righteousness'.

The prophet clearly had an intimate knowledge of the Psalms, and here he is foreseeing the joy of the scattered people of God gathering from around the world to enter Jerusalem, the sanctuary of the Lord.

The song includes the declaration of confidence in God who will keep watch over his faithful ones. But it also includes the exhortation to 'trust the Lord for ever', to trust God even when times are hard, for he will ensure that all things work together for the good of his beloved ones.

This passage is part of the end-time song of praise and thanksgiving. It affirms the experience of the believers who have come through the time of testing. They have proved the truth of God's promise that he will keep his beloved ones in perfect peace throughout the times of turmoil. The secret of this inner peace and serenity is that their minds are fully focused upon God.

The Lord is faithful. He can be trusted to keep his promises under all circumstances. Although the storm rages around us and we are buffeted and bruised, we will not be swept away because he is our Lord, and 'the Lord is the Rock eternal!'

Prayer

Today, Lord, we join with the great multitude of believers who have fought the good fight and come through the battle to dwell with you in eternity. As their songs of praise continually surround your throne, we now add our voice to their song. In the midst of the storm we praise you for filling us with your perfect peace. Keep me, O Lord, steadfast through this day.

LEARNING RIGHTEOUSNESS

Isaiah 26: 9-10

My soul yearns for you in the night; in the morning my spirit longs for you. When your judgments come upon the earth, the people of the world learn righteousness. Though grace is shown to the wicked, they do not learn righteousness; even in a land of uprightness they go on doing evil and regard not the majesty of the Lord.

Comment:

God's purpose in bringing his judgment on the nations is not retributive. It is not simply to punish and to inflict suffering. God wants to *save* people, not to destroy them. It is not his will that one single sinner should be destroyed. He is in the business of *salvation*, not destruction; of *giving* life, not destroying it!

The prophet expresses his yearning for God; night and day he finds himself longing to see the presence of God because he knows that God's purpose in bringing the nations to judgment is to establish standards of righteousness and to inaugurate a new system of world government.

Under the new system, men and women will no longer be driven by the forces of evil which lead to self-destruction. But they will be led by the Spirit of God into new life and joy and freedom.

The prophet sees that people react in different ways to the activity of God. When the Lord shows grace or loving mercy to wrong-doers, many do not respond by changing their ways. They scorn the grace of God. They go on doing evil 'even in a land of uprightness'. It is for this reason that the prophet longs to see the day of the Lord. He knows that

156

in that day, God will overcome the forces of evil that drive the nations and he will establish his reign of justice and righteousness.

Although many people do not respond to grace, everybody will have to respond to judgment. God has sworn a solemn oath to that effect: 'Before me every knee will bow: by me every tongue will swear' (see Isaiah 45: 23). Paul applies this to the Lord Jesus at his Second Coming: 'At the name of Jesus every knee shall bow... and every tongue confess that Jesus Christ is Lord' (Philippians 2: 10-11a).

This does not mean that they willingly accept Jesus, but that they cannot refuse to acknowledge his Lordship when he establishes his Messianic reign upon earth.

Some people are so strongly driven by a spirit of evil that their minds are closed to calls for repentance. Their ears are deaf to such appeals. They ignore all warnings that they are heading for personal disaster. They do not take any notice until the disaster actually comes. Then, in the midst of trouble, they are open to hear the word of God. When they are receptive to the Gospel they are able to receive God's love, mercy and goodness. Then, they are also able to receive the Spirit of the living God and to learn righteousness.

Prayer

Lord, make me sensitive to the promptings of your Holy Spirit. Speak, Lord, for your servant is listening. Deliver me from stubbornness and give me a willing spirit.

HONOURING THE LORD

Isaiah 26: 12-14

Lord, you establish peace for us; all that we have accomplished you have done for us. O Lord, our God, other lords besides you have ruled over us, but your name alone do we honour. They are now dead, they live no more; those departed spirits do not rise. You punished them and brought them to ruin; you wiped out all memory of them.

Comment:

This passage continues the song of praise, which is part of the end-times vision, which the prophet is describing in this chapter. It is central to the prophetic message that the freedom which the people of God enjoy, in the 'age of righteousness' that God will establish, is entirely due to God's action. It is stressed in our reading today that it is GOD who has established peace, not human beings.

In giving all the honour to God, the prophet goes even farther by saying that all that has been accomplished by the people of God has also been done by God working in and through them.

His witness is that others have ruled over God's people. He means both human beings and spiritual forces of evil. But God has now broken their power. They are dead; totally and finally defeated! In fact, their demise is so complete and the glory of God is so majestic and all-pervading that even the memory of them is wiped out.

This is how God will act globally when the time comes for him to judge the nations. But the wonderful good news that Jesus came to deliver is that he has already established the Kingdom of God on earth. The Kingdom, of course, will not be finally consummated until the last days. The good news is that believers are able, through the Lord Jesus, to enter Messiah's Kingdom now.

They do so, not through any righteousness of their own, but entirely through what God has done through Christ. This ensures that whatever we accomplish in this life we do it in his power and therefore all the glory is given to him.

Many believers could echo the words of testimony in this passage: 'O Lord, our God, other lords have ruled over us'. Indeed there are times in the life of even the most devout believer when we are not walking as close to the Lord as we would wish. There may be many reasons for this.

We can be oppressed by others around us or in our place of work. Bereavement, or a sense of injustice, or betrayal can leave us weakened and feeling that God is remote. It is at such times, when our hold on God is slipping, that his firm grip upon us brings us peace and security as he steps in to banish the powers of evil that seek to encompass us. He sets us free in the glorious liberty of his love that surrounds us all our days.

When we have an experience of the Lord setting us free, even from a period of dryness, we cannot restrain that leap of the Spirit within us. We simply have to say 'Praise the Lord, O my soul and all that is within me praise his name!'

Prayer
Lord Jesus, yours is the Kingdom, the power and the glory. May all that I do today be pleasing in your sight, O Lord. May my witness bring honour and glory to your name.

THE LORD'S DISCIPLINE

Isaiah 26: 16-18

Lord, they came to you in their distress; when you disciplined them, they could barely whisper a prayer. As a woman with child and about to give birth writhes and cries out in her pain, so were we in your presence O Lord. We were with child, we writhed in pain, but we gave birth to wind. We have not brought salvation to the earth; we have not given birth to people of the world.

Comment:

When God brings judgment upon the nations, the people of God also suffer. The believers are part of a nation. They are in the world even though they are already members of the Kingdom of God. They are citizens of two kingdoms, an earthly and a heavenly kingdom. So when the nation goes through a time of great testing, the believers also suffer.

In this passage the prophet is continuing to describe the end-times vision that he has seen. Clearly he is referring to believers, because he also begins in the third-person – 'they came to you in their distress'. Then he changes to the first-person-plural – 'so were we in your presence, O Lord'.

It is a lament for the powerlessness and ineffectiveness of the Lord's people in the face of the forces of darkness in the world. Despite all their efforts, they are unable to save their own country. They are incapable of bringing new life to the nation.

His illustration of the excruciating pain felt by a woman in childbirth is a vivid description of the distress experienced by the people of God when judgment comes upon the nations of the world. The prophet foresees them being in such a state of pain and shock that they can scarcely utter a word. Throughout their terrible experience he sees them unable to achieve anything truly creative. They are unable to produce new life.

The woman in labour is at least able to rejoice in the birth of a child, but the people of God are not able to produce anything worthwhile. Only God himself is able to save the nation and to bring new life and hope to all people.

There are times when each of us goes through great suffering, perhaps through the death of a loved one, or some other loss, failure or personal tragedy. The pain is so great that we can hardly even breathe a prayer before God. Life itself seems to lose all meaning.

At such times we have to rely completely, not on our own strength, or even on our faith, but entirely upon God's love and mercy.

This passage offers great comfort to those who are going through times of severe distress because it assures us that God does understand and that he will bring us through to a time of peace and rejoicing.

Prayer
Father, when we find it hard to pray, let your Holy Spirit intercede for us before your throne. Keep us close to your side when we go through times of great difficulty. Surround us with your love and uphold us by your strength.

RESURRECTION

Isaiah 26: 19
But your dead will live; their bodies will rise. You who dwell in the dust, wake up and shout for joy. Your dew is like the dew of the morning; the earth will give birth to her dead.

Comment:

This is a unique prophecy. It is the only reference from the mouth of any of the prophets of Israel to life after death. But this is not just a pious hope of some kind of post-death existence in the spirit world. In order to understand its significance it must be seen in context.

This prophecy is part of the 'end-time' scenario foreseen by the prophet. It follows the time of judgment, when God calls the nations to account, that began in Chapter 24. It comes to a wonderful climax in this declaration of faith that God will one day raise the dead to new life.

In this passage the prophet foresees a physical resurrection of the dead taking place, not in heaven, but on earth! It is a similar statement to that of Paul in 1 Thessalonians 4: 16f: 'the dead will rise first'. After that, Paul says, those who are still alive will join the Lord Jesus on his return to earth to establish his millennial reign.

Paul elaborates this further in 1 Corinthians 15: 20f where he describes Christ as 'the firstfruits of those who have fallen asleep'. He says, 'For as in Adam all die, so in Christ all will be made alive'. Revelation 20: 6 says that we will reign with Christ 'for a thousand years'.

The New Testament confirms the truth of this astounding prophecy in Isaiah 26 which was given hundreds of years before the birth of Jesus. For believers in

Jesus, this is part of the received tradition of our faith. Since the resurrection of Jesus, Christians have believed in life after death as part of the eternal life that is our inheritance in Christ. But for those living in the days of the prophets this was an entirely new revelation. It was left to Paul to explain about our new bodies when we 'shuffle off this mortal coil' and put on immortality (1 Corinthians 15: 52-54).

This is the sure and certain hope we have been given as believers in the Lord Jesus, our Messiah. We reaffirm the expectation of the resurrection of the dead and the coming Kingdom of God on earth every time we say the Lord's Prayer: 'Your Kingdom come, your will be done on earth as it is in heaven.'

The millennial reign of Christ is not just in heaven, but actually on earth – a transformed and renewed earth where sin has been conquered and death abolished. This is the climax of history that the prophet Isaiah was the first man on earth privileged to foresee!

Prayer
Lord Jesus, we praise you that you are the light of the world and the hope of all mankind. In you is life and immortality. We bless you for the assurance of life everlasting in your presence.

A SURE FOUNDATION

Isaiah 28: 16-17a
This is what the Sovereign Lord says: 'See, I lay a stone in Zion, a tested stone, a precious cornerstone for a sure foundation; the one who trusts will never be dismayed. I will make justice the measuring line and righteousness the plumb-line.'

Comment:

This is a prophecy to the rulers of Jerusalem. The exact dating is uncertain, but it was probably sometime during the reign of King Ahaz whose wickedness and idolatry are recorded in 2 Chronicles 28.

It was the unfaithfulness of Ahaz which led directly to a time of great suffering in Judah and defeat at the hands of Syria and Israel. The foreign policy of Ahaz was a disaster.

Judah refused to enter into an alliance with Syria and Israel against Assyria. But instead of putting their trust in the Lord which was the counsel of Isaiah, Ahaz turned to Assyria for help. This provoked the wrath of his neighbours and Judah was utterly humiliated by a combined army from Syria and Israel.

The Syrians took many prisoners to Damascus and in another battle Israel slaughtered 120,000 of Judah's army (2 Chronicles 28: 6). Israel also took as prisoners 200,000 women and children plus a great deal of plunder. But on their way to Samaria the prophet Oded strongly rebuked them for taking their brothers and sisters into slavery. The rebuke was heeded and the people were returned to Jericho.

The chapter from which our reading today is taken begins with a strong rebuke directed to Ephraim, the

northern kingdom, for their pride and debauchery. But
clearly Judah was no better! The rulers of Jerusalem
actually boasted that they had a 'covenant with death'
(v 18) an agreement whereby they would be spared when a
scourge swept across the land.

Isaiah had been shown that God was going to allow
judgment to come upon the whole land (v 22) because the
people were trusting in a false refuge (v 15). He heard God
saying that he was laying a precious cornerstone in
Jerusalem. It would be a sure foundation for the nation,
establishing standards of justice and righteousness. This
would be a foundation which would stand for all time and
those who built their lives upon it would never be
dismayed.

When we put our trust in the Lord, he is faithful to
guard our trust. He never breaks his promises to us. The
one essential is that we build our lives upon a sure
foundation.

St Paul reminds us that there is only one sure
foundation and that is Jesus Christ our Lord (1 Corinthians
3: 11). He is the chief cornerstone of the Temple of God.
When our lives are founded upon him, we are like a house
built upon rock, which even a violent storm cannot shift.
(See Jesus' parables in Matthew 7: 25.)

Prayer

*Lord Jesus, at the beginning of the day and in the evening I want
to acknowledge you. You alone are the sure foundation. In you
there is justice and righteousness. You alone are trustworthy.
Keep me close to you this day with my feet firmly upon the Rock.*

TIME TO SOW

Isaiah 28: 23-26
Listen and hear my voice; pay attention and hear what I say. When a farmer ploughs for planting, does he plough continually? Does he keep on breaking up and harrowing the soil? When he has levelled the surface, does he not sow caraway and scatter cummin? Does he not plant wheat in its place, barley in its plot, and spelt in its field? His God instructs him and teaches him the right way.

Comment:

This is clearly meant to be a word of encouragement. The words in our reading are part of a prophecy (vv 23-29) which stands alone. There is nothing to indicate its date of origin. The fact that it has been placed right after a pronouncement of judgment upon the whole land reinforces the view that it is intended to be a word of encouragement to the faithful. They are commanded to listen carefully and pay attention to the message.

The whole passage is based upon farming practice. This would be meaningless to rich city dwellers, so the inference is that the prophet is addressing a farming community, probably poor, working people who have been discouraged by adversity. Whether their suffering had been caused by problems with the harvest through drought or crop disease, or whether enemy armies had ravished the land, is quite unknown.

The message the prophet was conveying to the nation was that a time of judgment and suffering does not last for ever. His farming illustration is that the farmer does not go on ploughing the land and cutting it up for ever. His purpose in using the plough is to make the ground ready to receive the seed. Once it has been prepared, he ceases ploughing. Then it is time to sow.

In the next verse after our reading the farming illustration changes to harvest time. The prophet notes that a farmer does not go on threshing for ever. Once the wheat has been separated from the chaff it can be made into bread. The people can then enjoy good food.

Isaiah was emphasising that, although the nation was suffering in the midst of a time of rebuke, as soon as God's purpose of bringing the nation to repentance had been achieved, a time of blessing and rejoicing would follow.

God often uses adversity to prepare the way and to make his people receptive to his words. Ploughing breaks up the hard ground in our lives and opens us up to a fresh word from God. It shatters our complacency and makes us aware of having drifted away from God-centredness in our spiritual life.

When we go through times of adversity God often uses it to deepen our trust in him or to call us to repentance and to refreshing our love and trust in the Lord.

Prayer

Lord, help me never to be irritated by adversity, but to seek you humbly, to know what lesson you want me to learn. Thank you that in your mercy, adversity only lasts for a season! Grant me the joy of eating the bread you bring forth from the threshing.

TRUE WORSHIP

Isaiah 29: 13
The Lord says: 'These people come near to me with their mouth and honour me with their lips, but their hearts are far from me. Their worship of me is made up only of rules taught by men.'

Comment:

This verse comes in a chapter devoted to the city of Jerusalem. It begins with strong words of warning about an impending siege, although it also promises a great act of divine deliverance. God's most serious complaint against his people is that the prophets are asleep. Their eyes are blind so that they are unable to warn the people of danger. The prophets are powerless to bring the word of God to the nation.

When the prophets, or the preachers of the word of God, are asleep, or spiritually blind, the whole nation is in great danger. Clearly this was the situation in Isaiah's day. He heard the Lord saying the words of our reading today – 'these people come near me with their mouth and honour me with their lips, but their hearts are far from me.'

Their worship simply followed a pattern, or liturgy, made up by the priests and learnt by heart. It had become a meaningless tradition to be followed blindly. The people were routinely mouthing the words, but they were simply words, with no spiritual power or depth.

Neither the priests nor the people were really thinking about what they were saying. Therefore their worship was not honouring to God – it was simply routinised religion!

The whole nation was in danger because of the spiritual shallowness of their worship. Their religious leaders were spiritually blind and unable to teach the people the word of God. It was as though the whole nation, including the priests and the prophets, were playing charades. They were engaged in a kind of religious game which had the effect of keeping them from facing reality. Only Isaiah was aware of the true situation.

How easy it is to be lulled into a false spiritual state by religious routine! How often have we found ourselves in church saying familiar words of prayer, such as the Lord's Prayer, without really praying in our spirit? It is so easy to honour the Lord with our lips, but our hearts remain far from him.

There are times when we really need to hear this rebuke. We need to re-examine our prayer life and our whole attitude to worship. When was the last time you were, in the words of Charles Wesley, 'lost in wonder, love and praise'? Now is a good time to confess...

Prayer

...'I need you every hour most gracious Lord.' Save me from the dull routine of religion! Come, Lord Jesus, to revitalise my faith and to fill me with the wonder and joy of your presence. Help me to worship you with my whole life and not simply with my lips. Let today be special, Lord!

WHOSE PLANS?

Isaiah 30: 1-3
'Woe to the obstinate children', declares the Lord, 'to those who carry out plans that are not mine, forming an alliance, but not by my Spirit, heaping sin upon sin; who go down to Egypt without consulting me; who look for help to Pharaoh's protection, to Egypt's shade for refuge. But Pharaoh's protection will be to your shame, Egypt's shade will bring you disgrace.'

Comment:

Isaiah was vehemently against pacts and treaties with foreign powers. His message was quite simple – trust in the Lord, and in him alone! He was outraged to learn that Egyptian envoys were in Israel to negotiate a political treaty.

Isaiah was even more angry to discover (or possibly God had revealed to him) that the political rulers of the nation had negotiated a *secret* treaty! 'Woe to those', he cried, 'who go to great depths to hide their plans from the Lord' (29: 15a). The prophet poured scorn upon such futile actions because it is impossible to hide our deeds from the Lord.

The treaty no doubt involved trade as well as a military mutual-help alliance. Such agreements usually also carried certain spiritual implications. It was customary to acknowledge the gods of the nations with whom an alliance was made. This would involve the setting up of a shrine to the foreign god. Small nations such as Israel and Judah were put under great pressure to acknowledge the sovereignty of the gods of powerful nations.

To Isaiah, the setting up of such an abomination on the

soil of Israel was an insult to God, the Holy One of Israel, whose land it was. All the prophets regarded God, not simply as the God of the nation, but as having ownership of the land. Israel merely occupied the land as the husbandman of the Lord. They would only be permitted to do so as long as they were faithful to God.

For Israel to form an alliance with another nation was spiritual adultery; it was gross disloyalty to the Lord. It also meant breaking the covenant with God. The pro-Egyptian party had evidently persuaded the king to entertain Pharaoh's envoys and to enter into an alliance as part of their defences against a threatened Assyrian invasion. Isaiah denounced the plans saying they were not God's plans for his people and they would lead to 'shame' and 'disgrace'.

The existence of such an alliance was acknowledged by the Assyrian field commander in a letter to King Hezekiah when Sennacherib invaded the land. He said, 'Look now, you are depending upon Egypt, that splintered reed of a staff' (Isaiah 36: 6). Hezekiah had to repent of this and acknowledge that his only help was in the Lord, before God intervened to save Jerusalem.

When we make plans without consulting the Lord we put ourselves outside his protection. Repentance and turning to him in love and trust is the only way to be restored and to walk in the centre of his will for our lives. This often means taking large steps of faith, but God is faithful and he always honours such steps when they are taken in obedience to his word.

Prayer
Father, keep me back from making plans and asking you to bless them! Help me to consult you and to discern your will for my life and to walk in your ways.

REBELLIOUS PEOPLE

Isaiah 30: 8-11

Go now, write it on a tablet for them, inscribe it on a scroll, that for the days to come it may be an everlasting witness. These are rebellious people, deceitful children, children unwilling to listen to the Lord's instruction. They say to the seers, 'See no more visions!' and to the prophets, 'Give us no more visions of what is right! Tell us pleasant things, prophesy illusions. Leave this way, get off this path, and stop confronting us with the Holy One of Israel!'

Comment:

Isaiah was distressed at the sight of donkeys loaded with riches, and camels carrying some of the wealth of Israel to Pharaoh to seal an alliance with Egypt. The objective of the treaty was to establish a mutual-help military pact in the face of a threatened Assyrian invasion.

Isaiah had already declared this to be disloyalty to God and had said that it would bring shame and disgrace, not protection. But his counsel had not been heeded. His warnings had been ignored. In fact, he and his disciples had been told by the people, 'See no more visions! Give us no more visions of what is right!'

The people were not interested in prophetic warnings of disaster. They did not want to contemplate any other policy than the one the nation was following, which was giving them a comfortable lifestyle. They had got beyond caring whether it was right or wrong. They wanted the prophets to tell them 'pleasant things' even if they were an illusion. They were tired of being confronted with the Holy One of Israel.

Isaiah's reaction to this utter rejection of the divine counsel which he sought to bring to the nation was to write the message down. He had spoken it to his own generation, but the word of the Lord had been rejected, so now he was instructed by God to 'write it on a tablet' and to 'inscribe it on a scroll that for the days to come it may be an everlasting witness'.

It was necessary for future generations to know why disaster had struck the land. It was because the people were rebellious, and deceitful, 'unwilling to listen to the Lord's instruction'.

When we deliberately refuse to heed the word of the Lord, we put ourselves outside his protection. That should be obvious to all those who have given their lives to the Lord. But a more subtle danger is that of wanting to hear God say 'pleasant things' to us. We all like to hear good news, and we recoil from hearing warnings of unpleasant things.

The prophet who comes with a pleasant message, promising blessings, will always be popular. But he may be a false prophet, either deliberately, or (more likely) unwittingly, deceiving the people. It is in times of great danger that God raises up prophets to warn his people. He does not need to alert them to future blessings! Those who prophesy pleasant things are usually, although not always, giving illusions of their own minds.

Prayer
Lord, overcome my rebellious spirit and make me willing to listen to your word, even if it is not what I want to hear.

DEPENDING UPON DECEIT

Isaiah 30: 12-14

Therefore, this is what the Holy One of Israel says: 'Because you have rejected this message, relied on oppression and depended on deceit, this sin will become for you like a high wall, cracked and bulging, that collapses suddenly, in an instant. It will break in pieces like pottery, shattered so mercilessly that among its pieces not a fragment will be found for taking coals from a hearth or scooping water out of a cistern.'

Comment:

This is a very hard and uncompromising message which is difficult to date. It may have been spoken during the reign of Ahaz, but it is more likely to have been in the early years of his son Hezekiah. Although Ahaz cared nothing for the God of Israel, the record in 2 Kings 16 gives a graphic account of his idolatry with the gods of Assyria, but it makes no mention of a treaty with Egypt. Hezekiah, on the other hand, although given high praise by the historian in 2 Kings 18, is known to have concluded a treaty with Egypt.

Hezekiah is also known to have paid tribute to Assyria and then to have revolted against their rule. Later, when Sennacherib's army attacked Jerusalem, Isaiah was very supportive of the stand Hezekiah had taken. It is reasonable, therefore, to conclude that this strong prophetic warning was issued during the early years of Hezekiah's reign, probably about the time the Assyrians were attacking Samaria (724–721 BC).

Isaiah knew that it was wrong for Judah to rely upon Egypt. He knew that the very existence of such a treaty would spread complacency and a false sense of security. He was convinced that the only security was in God, and that security was now being jeopardised by reliance upon Egypt. In fact, Isaiah would have been against reliance upon anyone and anything other than the Lord. Hence the uncompromising warning in this prophecy.

The prophets always saw things in black and white. Things were either right or they were wrong. There could be no half measures and no watering down of the word of God. Isaiah's sense of outrage caused him not even to refer to the customary 'unless' – unless there were repentance this was what would happen. The situation was so urgent and the whole nation appeared determined to put their trust in Egypt. The prophet could see no alternative to utter disaster. He spelt out the consequences in no uncertain terms!

The picture of the 'high wall, cracked and bulging' was one that people would have instantly recognised. City walls were often built with several perpendicular structures with rubble between. The rubble was often mixed with rubbish which decomposed and expanded, thus causing a bulge in the wall. A bulge would have been a sign of corruption inside the wall which, if unattended, would soon lead to the collapse of the wall. Isaiah saw this as a parable of the nation where spiritual corruption would lead to national disaster.

In our own lives where corruption, injustice, or deceit lie hidden from view, the consequences will be severe. They cannot remain hidden from God. There is a build-up of pressure in our spiritual life that eventually leads to disaster. The only safety lies in real openness to the Lord.

Prayer

Lord, help me never to try to hide things from you. Help me to be open before you and may your Holy Spirit convict me of anything that is not pleasing in your sight.

QUIETNESS AND CONFIDENCE

Isaiah 30: 15-18
This is what the Sovereign Lord, the Holy One of Israel,
says: 'In repentance and rest is your salvation, in quietness
and trust is your strength, but you would have none of it.
You said, "No, we will flee on horses." Therefore you will
flee! You said, "We will ride off on swift horses." Therefore
your pursuers will be swift! A thousand will flee at the
threat of one; at the threat of five you will all flee away, till
you are left like a flagstaff on a mountain-top, like a banner
on a hill.' Yet the Lord longs to be gracious to you; he rises
to show you compassion. For the Lord is a God of justice.
Blessed are all who wait for him!

Comment:

This message continues the general theme of warning
against trusting in anyone or anything other than God.
Yet there is a softer note here than in the prophecies in the
first part of Chapter 30. Instead of straight condemnation, or
an unqualified warning of disaster, there is a note of sadness
and pleading in this passage.

The prophet sets out the answer to the main problem he is
addressing in this chapter. It is introduced as a direct word
from God and to emphasise its importance he stresses that
this word is from 'the Sovereign Lord, the Holy One of
Israel'. The message is that Israel's only salvation lies in
repentance and complete reliance upon God. Repentance had
to come first. There had to be an acknowledgment of
wrongdoing in the nation.

It was no good pretending that the nation was righteous.
Neither leaders nor people were trusting God. Repentance

did not simply mean acknowledging this, or just saying 'sorry' – but actually doing something about it as well! It meant turning away from disloyalty to God and putting full trust in him. Such an action would be rewarded with the power of God: 'In quietness and trust is your strength'. The AV uses the term 'quietness and confidence', which gives the sense of total expectation that God will be faithful to fulfil his promises.

Isaiah sees the rejection of God's promise of protection as tragic. The nation had turned its back upon the Lord and put its trust in horses and chariots – an army of cavalry. They were putting their trust in man and not in God! The consequences would be national defeat. The enemy would be too strong for them. Only God had the strength to protect them and he was longing to fulfil his covenant promises.

There is a note of pathos in the closing statement of this oracle, 'Yet the Lord longs to be gracious to you; he rises to show you compassion'. God was still willing to forgive and to draw his people back into close fellowship with him, because he is a God of justice. The Lord never abandons us even when we are unfaithful. He remains faithful always and is full of love and compassion for us when we fall into temptation. He longs to be gracious to us. So often, it is only our own stubbornness that creates the barrier and puts us outside God's protection. There is one simple answer to enable us to get back into the centre of his will – acknowledgment of our wrong-doing, or wrong attitude, and our great need of him; accompanied by an active turning away from sin, to obedience to God.

Prayer
Thank you, Father, that you are more ready to forgive than we are to repent. Thank you for your compassion for me in my weakness. Help me to find quietness and confidence in you.

THIS IS THE WAY

Isaiah 30: 19-22

O people of Zion, who live in Jerusalem, you will weep no more. How gracious he will be when you cry for help! As soon as he hears, he will answer you. Although the Lord gives you the bread of adversity and the water of affliction, your teachers will be hidden no more; with your own eyes you will see them. Whether you turn to the right or to the left, your ears will hear a voice behind you, saying, 'This is the way; walk in it.' Then you will defile your idols overlaid with silver and your images covered with gold; you will throw them away like a menstrual cloth and say to them, 'Away with you!'

Comment:

The circumstances of this prophecy are uncertain, but of its clear message conveying the love of God there can be no doubt. It reflects a time of suffering in the lives of the people of Jerusalem. It may well have been given during the time of great threat to the city when Sennacherib was laying a siege to Lachish and sent a threatening message to Hezekiah.

The account in 2 Kings 18: 4 says that Hezekiah cleared the land of any organised practices of idolatry. 'He removed the high places, smashed the sacred stones, and cut down the Asherah poles.' It records that he even 'broke into pieces the bronze snake Moses had made'. It seems incredible that this symbol, which had become an object of pagan worship, should have lasted in Israel for 400 years! It shows how deeply idolatry was embedded in the Hebrew culture.

Despite this official banning of idolatry, many people

still retained their household gods as this passage indicates. But Isaiah sees the day coming when the people will eagerly discard these as disgusting objects.

This is not a direct word from God, but it is a promise which the prophet has brought from the throne-room of God, from his times of intercession. It comes out of all his knowledge of the nature of God and his experience of the gracious and loving ways of the Lord. He is able to declare with confidence that, as soon as the people acknowledge their need of God and call out to him for help, God will answer.

The time of suffering that the people were enduring may well have been brought about by their own foolish actions or sinfulness. God sometimes allows his people to experience 'the bread of adversity and the water of affliction', but he never abandons us. The moment we cry out to him for help he is alongside us.

The day will come, Isaiah prophesies, when the word of God (his teaching) will no longer be hidden, or obscure. In fact, God will speak directly to his people. His word will be revealed to them.

This prophecy has been wonderfully fulfilled in the coming of the Lord Jesus who is the word made flesh. When we know Jesus as our personal Lord and Saviour, he is constantly at our side. When we turn from the right path he gently corrects us saying, 'This is the way; walk in it'.

Prayer
Father, sometimes our hearts are overwhelmed by your graciousness. Correct me, Lord, in your love and direct my steps throughout this day.

BINDING UP THE BRUISES

Isaiah 30: 23, 25-26
He will also send you rain for the seed you sow in the ground, and the food that comes from the land will be rich and plentiful. In that day your cattle will graze in broad meadows... In the day of great slaughter, when the towers fall, streams of water will flow on every high mountain and every lofty hill. The moon will shine like the sun, and the sunlight will be seven times brighter, like the light of seven full days, when the Lord binds up the bruises of his people and heals the wounds he inflicted.

Comment:

This is a lovely promise of blessing and prosperity. It is a promise that the labour of God's people will not be in vain. The seed which they sow will bring forth abundant food. Rain, in Israel, has always been seen as a sign of God's blessing and this is a promise to send rain in due season in order to ensure that the land produces food which will be 'rich and plentiful'.

The significance of this prophecy is that it does not envisage prosperity without pain. Clearly there was still a battle to be fought. The enemy had to be cleared from the land before the people could enjoy its rich produce. There would be a day of 'great slaughter' when the siege towers of the enemy would fall. But at that time, in the midst of the battle, God would be active. Streams of water would flow 'on every high mountain and on every lofty hill' to bless the land.

This was an assurance that God would be with his people. He would ensure that victory would be won and that a time of peace and prosperity would be established.

It is not certain whether or not this is a Messianic prophecy, but it has many such indications. It foresees streams of living water flowing across the land, and it sees great light shining, brighter than full sunlight. It also foresees God binding up the bruises of his people and healing their wounds.

This is how the Gospels present the mission of Jesus. The prologue of John's Gospel speaks of light coming into the world, 'the true light that gives light to every man' (John 1: 9). Jesus himself promised living water to all who would follow him. He said, 'the water I give will become in him a spring of water welling up to eternal life' (John 4: 14).

God does not promise that believers will be spared any of the troubles of life on earth. His promise is rather that he will never leave us alone. He is with us in the difficulties which we face, thus ensuring that we do not have to try to combat problems and opposition in our own strength. He gives both the strength and the guidance that we need.

This same promise is valid for believers today. When we are serving the Lord and we encounter opposition to the Gospel we can be sure that when the time is right he will destroy the 'siege towers' of the enemy.

He not only ensures victory, but he tenderly binds up the bruises which we have received and heals the wounds, especially those inflicted upon us by others whom we have loved and trusted. Such is the love with which he surrounds us at all times, even in the midst of the darkest hour.

Prayer
Lord, it is so wonderful that your presence turns the darkness into light. Help me to walk in your light throughout this day.

FLESH AND SPIRIT

Isaiah 31: 1-3a

Woe to those who go down to Egypt for help, who rely on horses, who trust in the multitude of their chariots and in the great strength of their horsemen, but do not look to the Holy One of Israel, or seek help from the Lord. Yet he too is wise and can bring disaster; he does not take back his words. He will rise up against the house of the wicked, against those who help evildoers. But the Egyptians are men and not God; their horses are flesh and not spirit.

Comment:

This passage rounds off the prophetic warnings against trusting Egypt. It repeats the warnings given in Chapter 30, but the emphasis is different. The charge here is not one of disloyalty to God by entering into pacts and treaties with a foreign power. Isaiah's central concern was that the nation was putting its trust in things of the flesh rather than of the spirit.

In going down to Egypt and seeking help from the armies of Pharaoh against the Assyrians, Judah was despising God. More importantly, the nation was making a fundamental mistake. They were trusting in the strength of flesh rather than in the strength of the Spirit of God. They were not looking 'to the Holy One of Israel' or seeking 'help from the Lord'.

In making a treaty with Egypt, the leaders of Judah thought they had made a good deal and that they had been wise in persuading Pharaoh to use the strength of his battalions of chariots for the defence of Israel. But they overlooked the fact that the wisdom of God destroys the 'wisdom of the wise'! (Isaiah 29: 14). As Paul put it some 700 years later, 'Has not God made foolish the wisdom of the world?' (1 Corinthians 1: 20). It was sheer stupidity to trust in the strength of men and horses rather than the strength of God.

The Lord had warned them not to run to Egypt; now the prophet not only reminded them that 'the Egyptians are men and not God; their horses are flesh and not spirit' but that God does not rescind his word. Once he has declared a word, it stands for all time. Thus in the day when God 'stretches out his hand' both Judah and Egypt would suffer.

This is a powerful message contrasting flesh and spirit. All the prophets constantly called for trust in the Lord rather than reliance upon man. The New Testament equivalent was Jesus giving his last instructions to the disciples. He warned, 'Do not leave Jerusalem but wait for the gift my Father promised.' Jesus added, 'In a few days you will be baptised with the Holy Spirit' (Acts 1: 4-5).

Jesus knew that if the disciples attempted to fulfil the Great Commission in their own strength, they would fail. He knew that they were eager to go out onto the streets of Jerusalem and give the astounding news of his resurrection from the dead. But enthusiasm alone would not have fulfilled the purposes of God.

We have to be just as careful today that we do not try to do the Lord's work with human strength. It is all too easy to be full of enthusiasm for the work and to forget to 'look to the Holy One of Israel'. It is only in the power of the Holy Spirit that we are able to accomplish the work to which the Lord calls us – not in our own strength but in his!

Prayer
Lord, guard me against relying upon flesh and not spirit. May the indwelling power of your Holy Spirit direct my steps today.

THE POWER OF GOD

Isaiah 31: 8-9
'Assyria will fall by a sword that is not of man; a sword, not of mortals, will devour them. They will flee before the sword and their young men will be put to forced labour. Their stronghold will fall because of terror; at sight of the battle standard their commanders will panic', declares the Lord, whose fire is in Zion, whose furnace is in Jerusalem.

Comment:

Isaiah had been giving strong warnings against trusting the Egyptians to defend Judah against an attack from Assyria. He constantly called for trust in the Lord. This prophecy is in verse form, but it is preceded by a piece of prose (31: 6-7) which is a call to return to the God of Israel from whom the whole nation, leaders and people, had turned.

The significance of this prophecy is that it follows all the warnings and calls for trust in God, with a direct promise that God will overthrow the Assyrians. This must have seemed incredible to the people of Judah who heard it. The Assyrian Empire was a mighty power that had overthrown every one of its neighbours in a relentless thrust to establish the dominance of Nineveh over the entire Middle East.

The modern equivalent of this statement would have been a prophecy foretelling the destruction of the mighty Soviet Union at the height of the 'Cold War' when the USSR appeared invincible. When the Soviets crushed the Hungarian uprising in 1956 their armies struck fear in the whole of Europe. That was the kind of fear that gripped the nations surrounding Assyria in Isaiah's day.

This direct prophecy that 'Assyria will fall by a sword that is not of man' was an expression of Isaiah's confidence in the

Lord. He knew that if God was calling for complete trust in him, he was planning a divine intervention. In the same way as he had promised Jehoshaphat that the battle was not his but God's, and he had overthrown the army that was attacking Jerusalem, so now God promised that he would destroy the attackers (cf 2 Chronicles 20).

The prophecy that promised divine action referred to the fire of the Lord in Zion and to Jerusalem being a furnace. A similar thought is found in Zechariah 12: 2 where Jerusalem is seen as 'a cup that sends all the surrounding peoples reeling'. Those who attacked the city of God would only harm themselves.

This word by Isaiah, promising that God would overthrow the Assyrians no doubt prepared the prophet for the time when the attack upon Jerusalem was accompanied by a threatening letter that was also insulting to God. When Isaiah heard its contents, claiming that God was no more able to save Jerusalem than the gods of the other nations had been able to save them, he immediately sought the Lord.

Before long he was able to send King Hezekiah a wonderful promise of deliverance saying that the King of Assyria would not be able to enter the city because God would defend it. The account in 2 Kings 19: 32-36 indicates that a great plague swept through the enemy camp decimating the Assyrian army and the remnant went back to Nineveh.

The power of God is sufficient for every situation. As Jeremiah says (32: 17), there is nothing too hard for the Lord! We will use his words as our prayer for today.

Prayer

'Ah, Sovereign Lord, you have made the heavens and the earth by your great power and outstretched arm. Nothing is too hard for you.' May your power protect your servants today.

EYES OPEN

Isaiah 32: 1, 3-4a, 5a, 6
See, a king will reign in righteousness and rulers will rule with justice... Then the eyes of those who see will no longer be closed, and the ears of those who hear will listen. The mind of the rash will know and understand... No longer will the fool be called noble... For the fool speaks folly, his mind is busy with evil; he practises ungodliness and spreads error concerning the Lord; the hungry he leaves empty and from the thirsty he withholds water.

Comment:

There is a clear difference between this passage and the preceding chapter of Isaiah. That is obvious even in the English translation. The reader who is familiar with the book of Proverbs and the message of the Psalms will recognise the influence of the Hebrew Wisdom Literature on this passage.

Yet there is also a clear intention of the prophet to relate this message to the theme of Chapters 30 and 31. This has led many scholars to refer to these verses as 'Wisdom Prophecy'.

The opening statement speaks of a righteous king establishing a reign of justice. It looks forward to the aftermath of the time of distress foretold in 31: 4-9 when God intervenes to bring salvation to his people. No longer will there be a hardening of the hearts of the Lord's people.

Those whose eyes are closed and whose ears are deaf to the word of God, will awake. Their minds will be alert with understanding in a manner that will be characteristic of the Messianic age. 'The mind of the rash will know and

186

understand, and the stammering tongue will be fluent and clear' (v 4). The presence of the righteous king will remove the cloud of confusion from the people and release the word of God to be declared among the nations.

This is a reversal of the first prophecy that was given to Isaiah following his call to ministry. He was told that people would be 'hearing, but never understanding ... seeing but never perceiving' (6: 9). The coming of the righteous king would reverse all that and take away the shroud of false teaching and deceit that hung over the nation.

The influence of the Wisdom Literature is to be seen in the reference to the fool. 'For the fool speaks folly, his mind is busy with evil.' The foolish person is the one who ignores God, who acts in a manner that does not take God into account.

The seriousness of this is that such people do not only practise evil themselves, but they 'spread error concerning the Lord'. This is the worst kind of sin for it is a direct offence against God. It is a lying witness.

When someone spreads false teaching, or encourages others to join a cult, or propagates some New Age teaching, they are denying the truth about God. They are thereby preventing those who are hungry and thirsty for spiritual food from receiving the nourishment for which they long.

We often do not realise the influence we have over others for which we are accountable before God. We should always guard carefully our witness to the truth.

Prayer
Lord, throughout this day keep my mind clear, guard my conversations and enable me to bear witness to the truth.

COMPLACENCY

Isaiah 32: 9-13a

You women who are so complacent, rise up and listen to me; you daughters who feel secure, hear what I have to say! In a little more than a year you who feel secure will tremble; the grape harvest will fail, and the harvest of fruit will not come. Tremble, you complacent women; shudder, you daughters who feel secure! Strip off your clothes, put sackcloth round your waists. Beat your breasts for the pleasant fields, for the fruitful vines and for the land of my people.

Comment:

This passage is a prophetic poem which acts as a bridge between the Messianic 'Wisdom Prophecy' at the beginning of Chapter 32 that we considered yesterday and the promise of future blessing with which the chapter concludes. We shall look at that tomorrow. The passage is addressed to the women, although its message is clearly intended for everyone! It is a solemn warning of impending disaster.

The warning was probably given by the prophet in a central area of Jerusalem, or possibly at a gate of the Temple, or inside one of the Temple courts. The women addressed are not the poor, but the well-to-do who were enjoying a lifestyle of privilege and security. It is this sense of security that the prophet attacks. He sees this as unwarranted complacency.

The prophecy of impending disaster has an element of precision – 'in a little more than a year you who feel secure will tremble'. The warning is about a military invasion that will overwhelm the nation. This is made clear in v 14 which refers to fortresses being abandoned and cities deserted. The effect of this military defeat will be such as to leave the whole land stripped and bare.

Isaiah directs his words to the women to give maximum effect to the warning because they were the ones most involved in the harvest festivities and they were the ones who led the mourning in bereavements and the lamentations in times of national disaster. They were instructed to take off their festive garments and replace them with sackcloth.

Jesus gave similar warnings against complacency. He urged his disciples to 'watch and pray', to be spiritually alert. It is all too easy to become complacent when we are feeling comfortable and secure in times of peace and prosperity. We become spiritually dull and unresponsive to the promptings of the Holy Spirit.

It is not the testing times of trouble which are the most dangerous, but the times when all is going well and we drop into self-satisfied complacency. It is at those times that we need to heed the prophet's warning.

Those are the times when our spiritual guard is down and we are most liable to fall to temptation. Pride and complacency often go together. We feel glad and self-satisfied when life is going well for us. We lower the great shield of faith, take off the whole armour of God as an unnecessary encumbrance. Suddenly, the enemy attacks and we are defenceless.

Prayer

Lord, guard me against complacency. Make me alert to what you are saying to me through your Holy Spirit.

THE FRUIT OF RIGHTEOUSNESS

Isaiah 32: 14a, 15, 17
**The fortress will be abandoned, the noisy city deserted...
till the Spirit is poured upon us from on high, and the
desert becomes a fertile field, and the fertile field seems
like a forest... The fruit of righteousness will be peace;
the effect of righteousness will be quietness and
confidence for ever.**

Comment:

This passage returns to the Messianic theme with which
Chapter 32 began. The national disaster foretold in the
previous verses had left cities deserted, fortified places
abandoned and the land trampled and neglected. Isaiah
foresaw all this happening as a result of the spiritual
complacency which had settled upon the nation and which
had made the people unaware of danger and impervious to
warnings.

The prophet saw the inevitability of the disaster
happening and he offered no hope of human strength or
wisdom being able to set things right. Quite the contrary,
he saw the disaster as a prelude to divine intervention. The
cities would be abandoned, the land would become
unfruitful and in mourning until the Spirit of God is
poured out from on high.

This promise of the coming of the Holy Spirit
foreshadows the more specific promise in Isaiah 44: 3 and
Joel 2: 28 which Peter quoted on the Day of Pentecost. This
is the first mention of the Spirit being poured out upon the
people. The image is that of a great outpouring of water
upon a parched and dry land which brings salvation to the
people and transforms the whole land.

This action of the Almighty in pouring out his Spirit from on high causes the desert to become a 'fertile field' thus affecting the whole natural creation. The most astonishing change is to be seen in people, in whose lives justice and righteousness will be established. In them, the fruit of righteousness will be peace. They will no longer be seeking to harm one another, but to bless each other. The effect of this righteousness will be a quietness and a confidence in God.

The age of the Spirit inaugurated by the outpouring of the Spirit of God upon all flesh means an end to war. The people will be continually blessed. This is the hope of Israel and 'the hope' to which Paul often refers in the New Testament.

While we look forward to the Second Coming of the Lord and the establishment of the Kingdom on earth, we need to recognise that the Kingdom has already been inaugurated through the advent of Messiah. We are therefore able to live in the quietness and confidence of Kingdom values through what the Lord Jesus has done for us.

The true believers in the Lord Jesus rejoice that they are actually able to live in the Kingdom right now. This is the heritage of the people of God.

Prayer

Father, I thank you for your great love and faithfulness. Enable me to live in quietness and confidence, trusting in your unfailing love and provision.

STRENGTH EVERY MORNING

Isaiah 33: 1-2, 5-6

Woe to you, O destroyer, you who have not been destroyed! Woe to you, O traitor, you who have not been betrayed! When you stop destroying, you will be destroyed; when you stop betraying, you will be betrayed. O Lord, be gracious to us; we long for you. Be our strength every morning, our salvation in time of distress... The Lord is exalted, for he dwells on high; he will fill Zion with justice and righteousness. He will be the sure foundation for your times, a rich store of salvation and wisdom and knowledge; the fear of the Lord is the key to this treasure.

Comment:

Chapter 33 begins with an end-times apocalyptic statement foreshadowing the rise of a world power which will rule the nations with ruthless savagery.

This world power is not identified, although Isaiah was writing against the background of the Assyrian invasion and destruction of Israel. It may be that he saw Assyria as a pattern of the 'world power' which would arise at some future date. This corresponds to the prophecy in Ezekiel 38 and 39 of the rise and fall of Gog and Magog who seek to dominate the world and who themselves come to destruction in the land of Israel.

Zechariah 12-14 is more explicit in showing that the climax of history will be reached when the nations attack Jerusalem. The city will become 'an immovable rock' and all who go against it will stumble and fall.

The same theme is repeated many times in the prophetic writings and becomes the central theme in the book of

Revelation where the final victory of God is assured.

In this passage the prophet first looks into the far distant future to reassure his people of the sovereignty of God and his almighty power to accomplish his purposes. He then moves swiftly back to the present which clearly is a time of considerable suffering for his people. He pleads with the Lord to be gracious to his people and to renew their strength, morning by morning. He acknowledges that salvation comes from God in times of distress.

Isaiah then makes a declaration of confidence in the Lord who is exalted far above the earth. The day will come when 'he will fill Zion with justice and righteousness'. He emphasises that the Lord will be 'the sure foundation for your times'. God is not only the God who holds the future of the nations in his hands, but he is also the one who cares for his people in the present times. He is a 'rich store of salvation, wisdom and knowledge'.

The key to all this treasure is 'the fear of the Lord'. This does not mean being afraid of God, but having a sense of awe in the presence of the Lord. It means respecting his Torah (teaching) and obeying his word.

Jesus told a parable about a man who discovered treasure in a field and sold everything to possess it. This is the kind of desire which all God's people should have towards this 'rich store'. It is there, within our grasp. We only have to reach out to the Lord to receive it, for he is longing to bless us by bestowing his treasure upon us.

Prayer
Lord, help me to enjoy your rich store of blessings today, and to move in your strength in the morning and throughout the day.

DWELLING ON THE HEIGHTS

Isaiah 33: 14-16
The sinners in Zion are terrified; trembling grips the godless: 'Who of us can dwell with the consuming fire? Who of us can dwell with the everlasting burning?' He who walks righteously and speaks what is right, who rejects gain from extortion and keeps his hand from accepting bribes, who stops his ears against plots of murder and shuts his eyes against contemplating evil – this is the man who will dwell on the heights, whose refuge will be the mountain fortress. His bread will be supplied, and water will not fail him.

Comment:

The apocalyptic theme is continued in this passage where God's action in defending Zion results in terror descending upon the enemies of Israel who have been attacking the Holy City. When God arises to fulfil his promises to his people, the wicked are destroyed and the ruthless nations are burned up.

The action of God also has an effect upon his own people. It makes them think of their own lives and wonder how they will be able to stand in the presence of Almighty God. The same question is asked in Malachi 3: 2 'But who can endure the day of his coming? Who can stand when he appears? For he will be like a refiner's fire or a launderer's soap. He will sit as a refiner and purifier of silver.'

It is the sinners in Zion who are terrified. Trembling grips the godless. They ask 'Who of us can dwell with the consuming fire?' Those who consciously break the covenant relationship with God and deliberately sin by disobeying his teaching are right to be afraid of his coming in judgment. The day will come when each one of us has to account for our own life before God.

Jesus said that when he comes again he will bring the nations before him and there will be a separation as a shepherd separates sheep from goats. Referring to the wicked, he said, 'They will go away to eternal punishment, but the righteous to eternal life' (Matthew 25: 46).

Having hinted at just such a teaching, Isaiah then emphasises the positive – the reward awaiting the righteous. He says that the righteous speak the truth, do not exploit other people, never accept bribes, refuse to have any part in violence and murder, and keep away from even 'contemplating evil'.

Those who thus live in a right relationship with God (the righteous) are likened to someone living high up on a mountain. Such a man or woman is in a protected fortress, kept safe by a loving God who also supplies all their needs. As God fed the prophet Elijah in the wilderness, so he supplies the food and water for his beloved ones. God longs to see each one of his children dwelling on the heights. That can be your experience today!

Prayer
Loving Father, good Shepherd of the sheep, guide me in the paths of righteousness this day and supply what is needful for me – no more, no less.

PAY ATTENTION!

Isaiah 34: 1-2, 4

Come near, you nations, and listen; pay attention, you peoples! Let the earth hear, and all that is in it, the world, and all that comes out of it! The Lord is angry with all nations; his wrath is upon all their armies. He will totally destroy them, he will give them over to slaughter... All the stars of the heavens will be dissolved and the sky rolled up like a scroll; all the starry host will fall like withered leaves from the vine, like shrivelled figs from the fig tree.

Comment:

Some Christians have problems with a prophecy of this nature that speaks of God being 'angry with all nations'. It does not seem to fit easily with some New Testament statements such as 1 John 4: 8: 'Whoever does not love does not know God, because God is love.' But the Bible rarely gives us simple cut-and-dried answers to matters of faith, especially in relation to the nature of God.

The revelation of God given to the prophets was that he is a God of love, compassion and tenderness. Hosea spoke of God taking his people in his arms and surrounding them with 'ties of love' (11: 1-4). He spoke of the conflict God experiences because Israel deserved harsh judgment for her wickedness. This conflicted with God's great love for his covenant people: 'All my compassion is aroused. I will not carry out my fierce anger … for I am God and not man' (11: 8-9).

The prophets nevertheless show that there are serious consequences to rejecting the word of God and ignoring the warnings that he sends. Within the nature of God there is both love and justice. The tension between these two comes to a climax in the Old Testament in the Suffering Servant of Isaiah 53 and in the New Testament with the Cross of Jesus. God enters into the suffering of those who respond to his love and takes upon himself the burden of sin in order to redeem those who put their trust in him.

This prophecy in Isaiah 34 is part of the end-times scenario in which God summons the nations to judgment before him. The whole passage has many echoes elsewhere in scripture.

Jesus speaks of his own Second Coming as a time when he will call the nations before him for judgment. He says, 'When the Son of Man comes in his glory … all the nations will be gathered before him' (Matthew 25: 31-32). He also says, 'The stars will fall from the sky and the heavenly bodies will be shaken' (Matthew 24: 29).

Similarly, Peter foresees that, 'The heavens will disappear with a roar' (2 Peter 3: 10). In the Book of Revelation, where there is a description of the coming of the four horses of the apocalypse, we read, 'The sky receded like a scroll, rolling up' (Revelation 6: 14).

God is a God of love and justice who hates the sin and loves the sinner. It may be because he knows the inevitable consequences of sin and where it will lead the nations that his warning here is so urgent. 'Listen; pay attention, you peoples!' This is surely what a loving parent would say to a wayward child.

It is a demonstration of the love of God who longs to save his children from bringing judgment upon themselves.

Prayer
Lord, break through the stubbornness of your people, including mine, and give us a listening ear.

BE STRONG! DO NOT FEAR!

Isaiah 35: 1-4

The desert and the parched land will be glad; the wilderness will rejoice and blossom. Like the crocus, it will burst into bloom; it will rejoice greatly and shout for joy. The glory of Lebanon will be given to it, the splendour of Carmel and Sharon; they will see the glory of the Lord, the splendour of our God. Strengthen the feeble hands, steady the knees that give way; say to those with fearful hearts, 'Be strong, do not fear; your God will come, he will come with vengeance; with divine retribution he will come to save you.'

Comment:

The whole of Chapter 35 is a prophetic poem. In the Hebrew it is beautiful poetry with a lovely message, following in strong contrast to the apocalyptic picture of divine judgment in the previous chapter, where God was seen as angry with all nations and with Edom in particular. The only link with that message is seen in verse 4 where the reference is to God coming with vengeance and divine retribution. But this was part of God's purpose in setting his people free from the persecution of their enemies.

Like all good story-tellers Isaiah withholds the punchline until the end of the poem. It is not until the last verse of the chapter that it becomes clear that he is talking about the return of the exiles to Zion. But there is a hint of this in verse 4 with the use of the Hebrew word *yavo*, 'he will come'. This is similar to Isaiah 40: 10: 'See, the Sovereign Lord comes with power'. Here it is linked with the exhortation to 'those with fearful hearts' to 'be strong, do not fear!' and the promise that God would save them.

The picture of the desert and the dry parched landscape being transformed into a paradise of natural beauty is one that has thrilled countless generations who have come to regard this as one of the most beautiful and best loved passages in the Bible.

The theme here is that of a well-ordered garden radiant with sunlight and bursting with a profusion of colour as a multitude of blooms combine to light up the landscape which was once bare and barren. It was as though the southern slopes of the Carmel range of mountains overlooking the vale of Sharon with its profusion of wild flowers was suddenly transported into the desert.

This, says the prophet, is what it will be like when the Lord comes to rescue his people from their persecutors. Those who had been taken from the land of Israel would one day be brought back. They would see the glory of the Lord preparing the way for them, and his presence would transform the whole land. Those who were suffering and fearful should feel comforted by this message.

In the past century, many parts of the land of Israel that have lain barren for centuries, are now literally blooming. It is a wonderful visual demonstration that the Lord fulfils his promises of restoration and new life.

This was a message meant to 'strengthen the feeble hands' and 'steady the knees that give way'. A similar message is given in Hebrews 12: 12. It is the promise of the Lord to all his people who remain faithful to him in times of stress, hardship and suffering. He is faithful to keep his promises and he will transform the desert in which so many of his people live into a beautiful garden radiant with the glory of his presence.

Prayer

Come quickly, Lord! Yavo *– he will come!*

WATER IN THE WILDERNESS

Isaiah 35: 5-7
Then will the eyes of the blind be opened and the ears of the deaf unstopped. Then will the lame leap like a deer, and the mute tongue shout for joy. Water will gush forth in the wilderness and streams in the desert. The burning sand will become a pool, the thirsty ground bubbling springs. In the haunts where jackals once lay, grass and reeds and papyrus will grow.

Comment:

The prophetic poem begun in verse 1 of this chapter continues the theme of the transformation of the whole of nature through the coming of the glory of the Lord. His presence changes not only the natural environment but also its inhabitants. 'The people walking in darkness have seen a great light, on those living in the shadow of death a light has dawned' (Isaiah 9: 2).

This was the promise given to Isaiah as he was permitted to look into the future to see the coming of Messiah and the establishment of the Messianic reign. The captives would be released from their persecutors, but so too would those who were prisoners to sin.

This is the meaning of the statement in Isaiah 42: 7 that the coming of the Messiah would open eyes that were blind and 'free captives from prison'. The effect of this would be to 'release from the dungeon' those who sit in spiritual darkness.

In the prophetic poem that forms our reading today we cannot dismiss the interpretation that the opening of the eyes of the blind and unstopping of the ears of the deaf means bringing enlightenment and truth to those who are deceived by false teaching and to those who have lost their faith in God and have turned away from the truth. Yet the description of the lame leaping like a deer and the mute being able to shout for joy surely means primarily physical healing!

The picture of the burning hot desert sand becoming a pool of water and the dry ground suddenly becoming the scene of bubbling springs of cool fresh water represent the total transformation of nature. Those who have suffered physical disabilities will have their bodies changed in the same way as the barren land becomes fruitful at the coming of Messiah.

Fresh water was always greatly valued in ancient Israel as indeed it is today in modern Israel. There is no more beautiful taste to the weary traveller than to drink from a fresh spring such as those up in the hills of northern Galilee and the Golan Heights where the Jordan rises. Jesus took his disciples there and often referred to water in a spiritual context.

On the last day of the great harvest festivities in the Temple Jesus called out to the crowds to come to him and receive 'streams of living water' (John 7: 38). That invitation is still there with the promise that all who come to him can be transformed here and now because, for those who believe in Jesus, the Messianic age has already begun.

Prayer
Lord, help me to enter more fully into the joy of your presence today.

THE HIGHWAY

Isaiah 35: 8-10
And a highway will be there; it will be called the Way of Holiness. The unclean will not journey on it; it will be for those who walk in that Way; wicked fools will not go about on it. No lion will be there, nor will any ferocious beast get up on it; they will not be found there. But only the redeemed will walk there, and the ransomed of the Lord will return. They will enter Zion with singing; everlasting joy will crown their heads. Gladness and joy will overtake them and sorrow and sighing will flee away.

Comment:

This is a beautiful conclusion to the final prophecy in the first part of Isaiah. The following chapters, 36 – 39, are historical narrative, the substance of which is found in 2 Kings 18f and 2 Chronicles 30f. The prophetic theme of this passage, which centres upon the return of the exiles, is resumed in Chapter 40. The build up of excitement and expectation continues throughout Chapter 35 and reaches a climax in the last verse heralding the arrival of the 'ransomed of the Lord' in Zion. They enter amid scenes of great rejoicing and festivities, surrounded with gladness and joy which dispels the 'sorrow and sighing' that has characterised the past.

There is no indication as to the location from which the ransomed are returning. In the time of Isaiah of Jerusalem in the Eighth Century BC the only exiles were those whom Sennacherib had deported from the northern Kingdom of Israel after the fall of Samaria. They were scattered across the Assyrian Empire in a deliberate attempt to destroy their national identity and to discourage revolt.

It was not until the time of Jeremiah some 150 years later that Jerusalem fell and large numbers from Judah were deported to Babylon. The seventy years of exile prophesied by Jeremiah ended in 520 BC when the Persians overthrew the Chaldean Empire and Cyrus issued a decree allowing the Judeans to go home.

It is not clear from this passage whether or not this is the event foreseen here. It may be that the prophet was seeing into the far distant future when Jews would be scattered all over the world. It may be that he was foreseeing in the last days a great return of the people of the Old Covenant to the land of their fathers. This would certainly fit the Messianic context of Chapter 34.

The prophet describes a highway that he sees in the vision he was given. It resembled a pilgrim's way which would be safe for the returning redeemed ones to walk without the fear of being attacked by robbers or men of violence.

The prophecy foresees a cleansed remnant who have come through times of great suffering but who now leave the sorrow and sighing behind them. They are full of the joy of the Lord, rejoicing in what he has done for them. Their arrival in Zion completes their pilgrimage of faith.

This is the promise that, through the Lord Jesus, the Father has opened the Holy City, symbolising the Kingdom, to all believers. It foreshadows the great bridal feast when all the redeemed are gathered into the presence of the Lord.

Prayer
Gather your people, Lord, from the farthest parts of the earth and fill them with the joy of your presence.

INDEX OF ARTICLES

ATONEMENT, THE 64
AWAY WITH HYPOCRISY 24
BANNER OF THE LORD, THE 128
BE STRONG! DO NOT FEAR! 198
BINDING UP THE BRUISES 180
CANOPY OF LOVE, A 38
CHOICE, THE 26
COMPLACENCY 188
CONSEQUENCE OF CORRUPTION, THE . . . 58
CURE FOR DECEIT, THE 52
DAWN WATCH 136
DEPENDING UPON DECEIT 174
DWELLING ON THE HEIGHTS 194
END OF IDOLATRY, THE 124
END-TIME PEACE 30
ENQUIRING OF GOD 84
EVERLASTING KINGDOM, THE 90
EYES OPEN 186
FALL OF BABYLON, THE 148
FEAR GOD NOT MEN 76
FIRE ALARM 96
FIRM FAITH 72
FLESH AND SPIRIT 182
FORGOTTEN GOD 126
FORMAL RELIGION 22
FRUIT OF RIGHTEOUSNESS, THE 190
GOD WITH US 74
GOD'S PROMISE 106
GOD'S PURPOSES 120
HE SHALL REIGN 146
HIGHWAY, THE 202
HOLINESS OF GOD, THE 62
HONOURING THE LORD 158
HUMBLING OF PRIDE, THE 32
INDEX TO HEADINGS 205
ISAIAH'S COMMISSION 60
JUSTICE OF GOD, THE 50
KINGDOM OF GOD, THE 122
LAST DAYS, THE 28
LEARNING RIGHTEOUSNESS 156
LIVING WITNESSES 82
LOOKING TO THE CREATOR 138
LORD'S DISCIPLINE, THE 160
LOVE OF GOD, THE 20
NATIONS IN HIS HAND 100

NATURE TRANSFORMED 112
NEW GROWTH 70
ON THE THRESHING FLOOR 134
PAGAN PRIDE 102
PARABLE OF THE VINEYARD, THE 40
PAY ATTENTION! 196
PEACE AT LAST! 132
PERFECT PEACE 154
POLLUTING THE EARTH 144
POWER OF GOD, THE 184
PRIDE AND ARROGANCE 92
PROMISE OF MESSIAH 108
QUIETNESS AND CONFIDENCE 176
REBELLIOUS PEOPLE 172
REJOICE AND BE GLAD! 152
RESPONDING TO GOD 66
RESURRECTION 162
REVERSING VALUES 54
RIGHTEOUSNESS AND FAITHFULNESS 110
ROBBING THE POOR 98
SECOND REGATHERING 114
SEEING THE LIGHT 86
SEVEN WOES, THE 48
SIGN IN EGYPT, A 130
SING FOR JOY 118
SPIRITUAL BLINDNESS 68
STRENGTH AND SALVATION 116
STRENGTH EVERY MORNING 192
STRONG WARNING, A 142
STUMBLING BLOCK 78
SURE FOUNDATION, A 164
THIS IS THE WAY 178
TIME TO SOW 166
TIME TO WEEP AND TIME FOR JOY 140
TRUE WORSHIP 168
TRUST IN GOD 104
VERDICT, THE 46
WAIT FOR THE LORD 80
WARNING SIGNS 34
WASHING AWAY THE DIRT 36
WATER IN THE WILDERNESS 200
WHAT MORE COULD I DO? 42
WHAT WILL I DO? 44
WHO ARE THE WISE? 56
WHOSE PLANS? 170
WIPE AWAY TEARS 150
WONDERFUL COUNSELLOR 88

In the same series:

Today With Jeremiah

Studies in the Prophecies of Jeremiah

This is a new approach to understanding the message of the prophet
Jeremiah. Dr Hill has spent many years studying the prophets. He sees
special relevance in the life and work of Jeremiah for today.

This is a series of daily readings in Jeremiah covering the first half of the
book. Each reading has an explanation of the message with an application for today. If you really want to understand the message of Jeremiah
for today this book will provide you with a feast that you will want to
read and reread.

'*Today with Jeremiah* provides a daily commentary on the book of
Jeremiah, explaining both the background and the meaning. Each day
the devotional challenge and application is highly relevant. I warmly
commend it.' *Viscount Brentford*

'Here in an accessible format for every concerned Christian is a clear
exposition of the main features of Jeremiah's teaching. In plain terms,
these pages help us understand the message and apply it to today's
world.' *David Anderson (from the Foreword)*

'To many, Jeremiah is the most human of all the prophets. He exposes
his angst and frustrations about his ministry in a way that is rare
amongst the other mouthpieces of God. Any serious commentary on
his prophecies, therefore, must integrate a study of his character with
a study of his words. This is exactly what Dr Clifford Hill does. These
studies are to be recommended for incorporating an analysis of the
man alongside a contemplation on his message.' *Bob Hunt, Vice-
Principal, All Nations Christian College*

*Available from Christian Bookshops and The Centre for Biblical and
Hebraic Studies, The Park, Moggerhanger, Bedford, MK44 3RW, UK.
Price £6.00 + £1.00 UK postage – ISBN: 1-872395-55-4*

PARDES

The Centre for Biblical and Hebraic Studies, also known by the Hebrew acronym Pardes, was formed in 1996 as a ministry of PWM Trust. Its aim is to enable Christians to study the Bible from an Hebraic viewpoint so that they may obtain a better understanding of its message.

This is achieved by means of residential and non-residential seminars, teaching days, special events, correspondence courses, study tours, celebrations of Jewish festivals and a range of resources including a quarterly journal, books, a bi-monthly teaching tape and other audio-tapes.

Please contact Pardes to request:

- information on the benefits of becoming a Member of the Centre
- the free regular bulletin with news of events and resources
- information about current correspondence courses
- details of the quarterly Journal
- a resource catalogue
- details about the bi-monthly teaching tape
- information about Hebrew language tuition and resources
- a speaker to come to your area
- details of how you can help financially with the work of the Centre.

Pardes may be contacted at:

The Park, Moggerhanger, BEDFORD, MK44 3RW
Tel: (01767) 641-400 Fax: (01767) 641-515
Email: pardes@the-park.u-net.com

PWM Trust

PWM Trust, incorporating PWM Team Ministries, *Prophecy Today* magazine, and the Centre for Biblical and Hebraic Studies, aims to bring the unchanging word of God to a changing world. The Trust has an international Bible teaching ministry with a particular emphasis upon the relevance of the Word of God today.

Prophecy Today is a bi-monthly magazine which examines contemporary world events from a biblical perspective. PWM produces a range of publications and tapes, promotes meetings on moral and spiritual issues and organises overseas study tours, particularly to places of biblical significance.

Please contact PWM to request:
- the quarterly PWM prayer and news letter
- a *Prophecy Today* subscription form
- a PWM resource catalogue
- details about the bi-monthly editorial update tape
- a speaker to come to your area
- details about how you can help financially with the work of PWM.

PWM may be contacted at:

The Park, Moggerhanger, BEDFORD, MK44 3RW
Tel: (01767) 641-400 Fax: (01767) 641-515
Email: pwm@the-park.u-net.com